WORLD WIDE SERIES

General Editor: James L. Henderson
Senior Lecturer, Institute of Education, London University

WORLD

POPULATION

MICHAEL PALMER

Deputy Headmaster, Littlehampton School

B. T. BATSFORD LTD London

First published 1973
©*Michael Palmer* 1973

Typeset, printed and bound in Great Britain by
REDWOOD BURN LIMITED
Trowbridge & Esher
for the publisher B. T. Batsford Ltd, 4 Fitzhardinge Street, London W1A 0AH
ISBN 07134 1581 9 ✓

ACKNOWLEDGEMENT

The author and publisher wish to thank the following for the illustrations which appear on the pages indicated: Associated Press for page 85; the Australian News and Information Service for pages 56, 58; the Trustees of the British Museum for page 11 (Natural History Dept), page 13 (Map Room), page 64 (Dept of Prints and Drawings); B. T. Batsford for pages 10, 29, 31, 40, 51, 52, 71 (right), 76, 93; Camera Press for pages 67, 82, 84; Christian Aid for page 65; Courtaulds Ltd for page 92; FAO for pages 37, 62, 69, 75 (bottom); Prof von Fürer-Haimendorf for page 25; Greater London Council for pages 43, 49; Heal and Son Ltd for page 41; IAEA for pages 68, 96; ILO for page 9; International Planned Parenthood Federation for page 32; the Israeli Embassy for page 70; the Imperial War Museum for page 54; the Japanese Information Service for page 15; Keystone Press for pages 20, 23, 46, 89; Michael Lattimore for page 16; the Mansell Collection for pages 12, 60; the Milk Marketing Board for page 75 (top); the Ministry of Works for page 6; Lady Morley for page 27; Renault for page 55; Rex Features Ltd for pages 47, 81; the Science Museum for page 8; the *Times* for page 19; UNICEF for page 79; USIS for page 87; WHO for pages 35, 36, 71 (left), 73, 77.
They also wish to thank publishers who gave permission for their material to be used as the basis of the diagrams on pages 17, 29, 44 and 57, where their names appear. The illustrations were collected by Illustration Research Service Ltd.

CONTENTS

FOREWORD

Growing up in the second half of the twentieth century means being globally involved and committed. However localised the lives we lead, these are increasingly influenced by forces which cut right across the traditional divisions of nation, class, race and creed. That is why World Wide has been chosen for the title of this series. Each volume in it, after Sheila Gordon's general introductory one, *World Problems*, deals with one aspect of the contemporary human scene. It is hoped that these illustrated studies will make an educational contribution to the solution of the problems of mankind's emerging world order.

Readers of this book, now aged fifteen to twenty-five and living in a world of some 3,700 million human beings, will find themselves members in their middle age of a world community of over 7,000 million. The reasons for this astonishing fact are clearly set out in the following pages. Although they are stated in no sensationally alarmist manner, their implications are alarming and alerting. 'There is a world population problem,' remarks the author, 'but it takes on a different form in each part of the world'. He demonstrates this first by making the point that population growth on this vast scale is a very recent phenomenon: 200 years ago there were less than 800 million inhabitants of the globe. Then he proceeds to explain how the population size is recorded and how birth and death rates may be controlled; he provides three strikingly contrasted case studies – the United Kingdom, Australia and India and then relates population control to land use and food production.

To provide the rising generation of both developed and developing countries with the necessary basic information to enable them to master this world population problem is an educational imperative: the following pages do just that.

James L. Henderson

1 INTRODUCTION

THE PROBLEM OF POPULATION

Population growth is one of the most worrying aspects of human existence at the present time. World population was 3,617 million in 1972 and if the present rate of growth is maintained there will be over 6,000 million by AD 2000. If this rate of growth continued for 700 years there would be one person for every square metre on the earth including both sea and land. The prospect emerges of a people who live under the earth, so that space can be found for food production.

Such projections of population and the consequent forecast of a disastrous fall in the quality of human life are pure guesswork. They are not the main concern in this book. The changes in world population in the last 200 years are without parallel in human history. Rapid population growth has occurred before, but always in a small area and for a short period of time. What makes the present growth of population unique is that it has been sustained over a long period and is now progressing on a world scale.

Before the Industrial Revolution it was the experience of most communities that a period of rapid population growth was succeeded by some natural disaster in the form of starvation or disease. It is therefore tempting to suppose that such a cycle will occur again to check the present world population. This may be the case in some instances, but it would be unrealistic to predict such a catastrophe on a world scale. The speed and nature of population growth differs from area to area. In some cases population growth is moderate enough to stimulate a community to greater production and increasing prosperity; in others population growth is fast but not as fast as the growth of the food supply. It is only in the minority of cases that the population growth outruns the supply of food with catastrophic results. This book seeks to examine the many forces which affect population and to suggest relevant solutions. There is a world population problem, but it takes on a different form in each part of the world.

PRIMITIVE SOCIETIES

It is increased food supply that has made the rise in world population possible. The first men lived off wild berries, fruits and any small animals that they managed to kill. This would have been over a million years ago. For most of his existence on earth man refined his hunting and fishing techniques so that he could feed more amply off the profusion of nature. While he lived off the land in this way as a primitive hunter, the human population remained very low, as it took a large area of forest to support one family. At the end of most of the million years of human existence, world population was no more than twenty million people. It is only in the last 10,000 years that agriculture has been practised and it has made possible a large increase in the food supply.

Agricultural change has occurred in two main phases. The first change was the introduction of farming by the New Stone Age people in the Middle East around 7000 BC. Communities in the area of Palestine and the valleys of the Tigris and Euphrates began to domesticate animals and to sow barley and wheat with the

Early settlement in Scotland, 1000 BC. The foundations of an early agricultural settlement have been preserved beneath the sands of the coast. A small community like this would have been capable of grazing animals and cultivating the light coastal soils.

intention of reaping the crop. The art of farming spread from there into Europe to reach Britain about 2000 BC. The discovery of farming seems to have been made independently on the American continent. Specimens of domesticated maize have been discovered by archaeologists in Mexico, which have been dated by radio-carbon to before 3000 BC.

New Stone Age farming was 'subsistence' farming in the sense that food was only provided for the farming community itself. It sustained a gradually increasing population, but the techniques of farming did not improve enough to provide a guaranteed surplus for sale. There were surpluses in places of natural fertility like the Nile delta, where grain bins dating from 4500 BC have been discovered, but in the forests and meadows of Europe farming only provided for the community itself. The German races contributed to agricultural technique by inventing a system of tillage appropriate to the heavy clay lands of Northern Europe. They developed in particular a heavy plough drawn by eight oxen and equipped with mould-board and coulter to turn the sod, instead of scratching the soil as the Mediterranean ploughs did. This plough was introduced into England by the Anglo-Saxons and enabled them to colonise the fertile valleys.

AGRICULTURAL SOCIETY

The population of the world was about 750 million in AD 1760. There had been a steady rise in population in most European and Asian countries since the fall of the Roman Empire which accounted for a trebling of world population between AD 350 and AD 1760. Almost all of the increase occurred in Europe and Asia. America was still a more or less empty continent, much of it peopled by primitive Indians at very low population densities. There were more advanced civilisations in Mexico and Peru but neither was in a very favourable agricultural area.

European colonisation of North America on the eastern coast increased the population after 1600 but there were still only about 2 million people in the USA and Canada in 1760, because the prosperity of the European colonists was matched by the decimation of the native Red Indians from European diseases, to which they had no natural resistance. This was the fate of most primitive tribes when subjected to contact with the European world. Australia was still virtually empty in 1760 except for the wandering aboriginal tribesmen, while Africa had a population of around 100 million.

The only areas to show a decline in population between AD 350 and 1760 were Asia Minor and North Africa. This is clearly connected with the decline of the Roman Empire in the Mediterranean area and of the older civilisations in Western Asia. It seems that Persia and Egypt supported a larger population before the Roman conquest of the Eastern Mediterranean than during it. The Sumerians and Babylonians depended on sophisticated schemes of irrigation and flood control that went into decay when the civilisations were overthrown. The badly-maintained ditches and areas of marsh may have provided the stagnant waters for the malarial anopheles mosquito. It is thought that malaria may have been the cause of population decline.

Egypt was the granary of the Roman Empire, yet there is written evidence that pressure on the land was not great during the Roman occupation. There was a significant decline of population in Egypt after the collapse of the Roman Empire in Europe in the fifth century, from which there was no real recovery until the nineteenth century.

The end of the Roman Empire was marked by a sudden fall in population in Europe also. The Roman towns and cities were ignored by the barbarian tribes that marauded into Southern and Western Europe from Asia. Trade virtually ceased once the Muslims occupied North Africa and the Roman roads fell into disuse. Europe reverted to an almost totally agricultural economy, organised for subsistence only.

There was no great recovery of cities and trade until after 1050. By this time the Vikings had opened up trade links between Northern and Southern Europe and the establishment of a crusading kingdom in Syria and Palestine had reopened links with the East. The economy of Europe became much more varied as a result and great cities in North Italy and Flanders began to grow. The recovery of trade was matched by a rapid growth of population, reaching a peak in 1348. During the years between 1050 and 1350 the population of Europe doubled and in some areas trebled. One of the high growth areas was Britain and there is evidence that during this period much poor agricultural land was occupied. This was particularly the case on the chalk wolds of Leicestershire where the soil layer is too thin for easy arable farming. Many

(*Above*) Heavy plough. This is the kind of plough that was developed by the German races to enable them to farm the heavy clay lands of Northern Europe. The knife-like coulter cuts the ground, while the mould-board undermines the turf and throws it over.
(*Opposite*) Pickaxe cultivation. This kind of implement was used to cultivate the light upland and coastal soils before the introduction of the heavy plough. The early plough was a spike which scratched the surface. These primitive implements are still used in many under-developed countries. This picture was taken in Tanzania.

Evidence of a deserted village. There are many such deserted sites in the English Midlands and North. Communities which produced cereals on the thinner soils during the Middle Ages were often disbanded to make way for grazing once sheep-farming became profitable in the fourteenth and fifteenth centuries. Other communities succumbed to the Black Death in the middle of the fourteenth century and never recovered. The plots and tracks of many of these villages still remain imprinted in the grassland on which sheep have grazed for centuries. This is the deserted village of Wharram Percy in Yorkshire, where little apart from the church remains.

communities settled there in the thirteenth and early fourteenth centuries and ploughed the chalk, but they soon disappeared. All that remains of them and hundreds of other medieval villages settled in unfavourable areas at this time are a few grassy humps and a pattern of tracks in the turf which mark a deserted village. There are sixty such sites in Leicestershire and a similar number in many other Midland counties. Most of them subsequently reverted to sheep farming for which the terrain was much better suited. Sheep farming needs very little labour and was also very profitable. A writer in 1548 expressed the view that 'grazing requires small charge and small labour which in tillage consumes much of the master's gain'.

The event which threw most communities off balance was the visitation of the Black Death in 1348. This was the first of many outbreaks of bubonic plague and it cut down the population of England by one third. The Black Death had a similar effect on all the countries of Western Europe and proved the worst catastrophe in European population development. English population did not recover to its former size until around 1600, by which time there was scholarly talk of England being overpopulated. It was felt that the solution was to settle colonies in the New World.

The argument that England was overpopulated in 1600, with a population of just under four million, was not far-fetched. Agricultural prices were high and it seemed that population was growing quicker than food production. The land had

A black rat. This is the plague rat which made way for the brown rat in the eighteenth century. As houses became cleaner the black rat was driven out into the open, where the brown rat was much better equipped for survival. The black rat gradually disappeared and with it went the host flea, which was the main plague-carrier. The decreasing occurrence of plague can be directly attributed to the black rat's disappearance.

to provide most of man's daily needs. It had to provide barley for ale as the basic drink, fuel for the fire, timber for ships and houses, wool for clothing, fodder for horses as the main form of transport, hides for shoes and animal fat for candles as the basic form of lighting. On top of all this, areas were also set aside for the main aristocratic pleasure of hunting. In these circumstances, pressure on the available land had become too great and it was necessary to exploit land resources more effectively if the increased population was to be adequately fed.

Pressure on land was relieved by the increased use of coal as a fuel and brick as a building material, but a new threat to the forests developed with the growing use of wood for charcoal burning in the production of iron. The changes which helped to improve agricultural production in the seventeenth century were the drainage of the Fens, the introduction of new crops like clover and turnips and an interest in more scientific farming. Population continued to rise steadily in the wake of these improvements, while the incidence of plague began to decline. One of the last great outbreaks was the Plague of London in 1665.

The disappearance from Europe of the plague as the main check on population growth was connected with the replacement of the black rat by the larger and fiercer brown rat from Scandinavia. The grey rat began to move southwards in the early eighteenth century and took over the black rat's habitat in houses and shops. Contemporaries knew nothing about the importance of this change, which was only discovered after some very minute recent scientific investigation into the causes of plague. Plague is in fact carried by one species of flea, which is happy to live in the fur of the black rat, but will only live in the nest of a brown rat. The smaller black rat preferred to find a home inside people's houses, while the grey rat had much more wandering habits with its nest often outdoors. As hygiene improved with the displacement of wattle and daub by brick, of thatch by tile and of rushes on the floor by carpets, the black rat found its normal habitat disturbed. Once the grey rat arrived in England around 1728, it drove away the black rat altogether.

In almost all European countries, population grew more rapidly in the eighteenth century than previously. Population tended to grow by about one per cent per year in pre-industrial societies but this rate of growth was normally cut back by epidemics, harvest failures or wars. In England at least, not only did epidemics decrease in the mid-eighteenth century but also it was the time when there was a succession of good harvests from 1730–55. The growth of population that resulted was easily absorbed as extra labour by the new factories and developing industry was able to satisfy the demands of growing population.

There was also a radical change in agricultural methods during the eighteenth

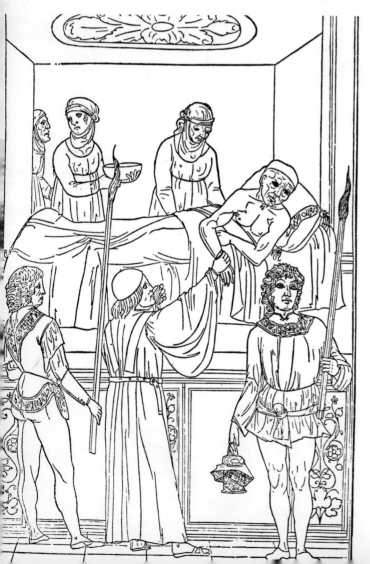

Tending a plague victim. This print dating from 1493 shows a plague victim being tended by a doctor. The doctor is smelling an amber apple. This was supposed to keep him from infection. Plague was always liable to break out while the black rat roamed free in people's houses.

Norden's map of Sussex, England. This map of Sussex was drawn in Elizabeth's reign (1558-1603) when it was felt by some that Britain was becoming overpopulated. The forests were being cut down to provide wood for iron-making and the fertile ground was occupied extensively. Scholars could not see where more people could be settled except in new colonies overseas.

century, as most farmers began to produce a surplus to feed the growing towns. Scientific stock breeding, the use of new crops for cattle feed, the consolidation of farms and the end of the fallow field system all helped to increase food production in such a dramatic way that the rapidly growing town populations were not only fed but began to enjoy a better diet than before. The improvement of agricultural output has been sustained since that time with the help of machinery and artificial fertilisers so that in those countries that have experienced an agricultural revolution, population has not only increased greatly but enjoys an ever-improving standard of living.

INDUSTRIAL REVOLUTION

There is a continuous debate among economic historians about whether population growth generated the Industrial Revolution or whether the Industrial Revolution generated population growth. There seems no doubt that the sustained English population growth in the mid-eighteenth century did stimulate industry and agriculture to increase output, but once industry started the headlong expansion described as the Industrial Revolution, population began to rise even more quickly.

At the end of the eighteenth century population not only increased, but began to increase at a continuing high rate, so that by the turn of the century it was increasing at nearly 1.8 per cent per annum. Despite the rapidity of the increase to a peak about 1820, the improvements in industry and farming enabled the larger population to enjoy a gradually improving standard of living.

Britain was the first country to experience an Industrial Revolution, but it has since been followed by most European countries, by most of Europe's former colonies and by Japan. Cottage industry was replaced by factory industry centred on large towns; transport was developed to carry raw materials and manufactured products; the growing population provided the labour force needed by industry; improved wages enabled people to buy more manufactured goods; increased agricultural production and the importation of foreign agricultural products satisfied the growing demand for food. This brought about the change from an agricultural to an industrial economy.

World experience suggests that industrial production and agricultural production are able to keep ahead of population growth, so that the quality of life for the average person steadily improves. Such growth of production cannot go on for ever as the productive capacity of the soil is not inexhaustible.

As far as Britain is concerned there was a progressively sharp decrease in family size between 1870 and 1930 to a point where there was serious concern at the possibility of a declining population in the future. It did not happen, as there was a slight increase in the average size of family in the late 1930s which continued after the Second World War. What recent experience of population growth does demonstrate is the tentative nature of forward forecasts. It needs quite a small adjustment of average family size either upwards or downwards for the future pattern of population to change completely.

WORLD EXPERIENCE

The pattern of population growth in the non-industrialised world has been very different, mainly because it has experienced a population growth without an Industrial Revolution. Agricultural and industrial production have only managed to keep pace with population growth and consequently, although population has risen, the standard of living has remained the same. India, in the main, has remained an agricultural economy where the increased population has stayed in the villages. When Indian peasants move into cities like Calcutta, they merely add to the number of beggars as there is no growing industry to provide employment for them.

The equivalent European experience was that the increased population was partly absorbed on the land, where increased production was at first dragged from the soil by a more intensive use of labour and partly in the new industrial towns. On balance, in Europe, the proportion of people living in towns has steadily increased. This is because machinery began to be used for more of the work on the farms, making farm labourers unemployed. These people moved into the towns to find jobs. In the undeveloped world, on the other hand, the proportion of people living in towns increases only very slowly.

Road system in Tokyo. Japan was quick to adopt the systems of the most advanced industrial countries and is now outpacing them in many respects. Apart from the road signs, this could be a scene in any city of Western Europe or North America.

Until more productive jobs can be provided for Indians, Chinese and others in a similar state of economic development, they cannot be paid higher real wages; without such wages they cannot buy goods which will improve their standard of living, and so there will be no reason for industry to manufacture them. The end of this vicious circle is that without a stimulus to increase its output, industry will not provide more productive jobs and without these there will be no incentive to move into the towns to find work. Many nations in South America and Asia face this problem and if they cannot find a solution to it, nature will find its own solution in increased deaths from malnutrition and deficiency diseases.

Japan's experience has been exceptional as an Asian country that has experienced an industrial revolution. The situation seemed by no means favourable in the middle of the nineteenth century. Japan had been experiencing a steady growth in population from twenty-three million in 1650 to thirty million in 1850, but the population seemed to have reached a plateau in what has been called a period of 'famines, epidemics, abortion and infanticide'. The government in power, a family oligarchy called the Tokugawa Shogunate, was bent on isolating Japan from the rest of the world and on stabilising the political system on the generally accepted basis of agriculture and even more narrowly on rice production. Yet once the Shogun were overthrown and the Emperor Meiji restored in 1872, Japan quickly adopted Western government, industrial capitalism and technology with such rapidity that by the turn of the century the Japanese economy had been transformed.

At the same time the Japanese attitude to family size changed with equal rapidity and they began to produce some of the largest families in the world. There was in fact a 25 per cent increase in the Japanese population between 1894 and 1914. The average size of the Japanese family began to moderate in the 1920s and the most recent information in 1960 was that a family of only two children was in greatest favour even though Japanese industry continues to expand at a very fast rate of 9 per cent per annum.

China has the largest population in the world but it remains substantially an agricultural economy. Since the Communist Revolution in 1949, vigorous attempts have been made to overcome inertia, but an industrial revolution has not been achieved. Attempts have been made to organise industry in the fields with back-yard blast furnaces, and to move labour from the fields into the factories, but it has proved impossible to change the traditional peasant outlook in one generation. It is to be

Backyard furnace of the 'Great Leap Forward' period in China (1958). The Chinese Communist Government tried to use the surplus manpower in the countryside to produce industrial raw materials. This kind of blast furnace could be set up in any village where iron ore was available.

expected that central planning will in the end move China's bountiful labouring force into more productive pursuits, but this will take time.

Many countries in the underdeveloped world face similar problems to China. Fertility is still as high as it always has been, yet mortality continues to decrease with the application of modern medical knowledge. Nothing except an abnormal catastrophe could reverse the growth of population for at least two generations, for the large, recently-born generation is bound to produce many children of their own even if they have smaller families. For this reason radical measures are needed if a solution to the short-term problem of numbers is to be solved. In the longer term, it is to be hoped that fertility will decrease to conform more closely with the declining mortality.

Population Sizes

Argentine	1964	22,038,000	France	1967	49,548,000
Canada	1967	19,933,000	Italy	1966	53,128,000
Mexico	1966	44,145,000	Spain	1967	32,431,000
USA	1967	197,863,000	Sweden	1967	7,868,000
Venezuela	1965	8,722,000	United Kingdom	1966	54,600,000
			USSR	1957	208,827,000*
China	1967	710,000,000*			
India	1961	439,235,000	Australia	1967	11,810,000
Indonesia	1961	96,371,000	New Zealand	1967	2,729,000
Japan	1966	98,859,000			
Pakistan	1961	93,832,000	Nigeria	1961	34,174,000*
			South Africa	1957	14,167,000

* *estimate*

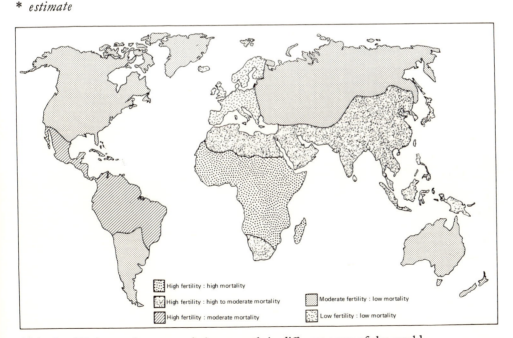

This simplified map shows population growth in different parts of the world.
(Map adapted from *Man and His Environment*, 1965, BBC Publications, after a diagram in *Our Developing World* by L. Dudley Stamp, Faber and Faber Ltd.)

2 METHODS OF MEASUREMENT

The study of population is a subject in its own right with its own methods of measurement and its own terminology. The study is called *demography* and the aim of demographers is to measure the size, growth and contraction of human populations and in particular the part played by fertility and mortality in population changes. The main purpose of the study is the same as that of any other scientific investigation, and that is to find patterns in the confused and complicated data that they are studying. In the case of demography, the search is for trends and patterns in the most basic activities of man: birth, reproduction and death. The results of the demographers' researches are very useful in the prediction of future human needs. It is vital to have some idea of how many children will need educating in ten years' time when planning schools, or what the chances are of a man's survival when offering him a life assurance policy. The more complicated society becomes, the more it becomes necessary to plan ahead for human needs.

CENSUSES

A census involves the simple counting of heads. Such counts were made from very early times for some limited purpose such as tax-collecting or military service. They concentrated on the male adults and the results were usually kept secretly for government use. The object of the modern census is very different. It is equally interested in everyone, however young or old and whatever their sex, for the aim is to accumulate the statistics necessary to predict both the present and the future shape of society. The information is published for the use of government officials, economists and social workers in their work of forward planning.

A count of this kind is a very difficult operation and can only be attempted by a fairly advanced state. Complicated forms have to be used which means that either the majority of the population have to be able to read and write or the government have to employ an army of enumerators to carry out the count over a very short period. Ideally the count should be made at one particular moment of one particular day, otherwise people with no fixed home may well escape the count or for one reason or another be counted twice.

A simultaneous count can be achieved quite easily where the community is neatly settled in households and most people can write, but it is virtually impossible in an agricultural community where a home may be a tent or a temporary shelter. As a result of the expense and difficulty, one-third of the world still is not counted regularly and another third is not counted as accurately as demographers would like.

The first modern census in Britain was held in 1801 and since that time one has been held every ten years, except for 1941 when it was cancelled due to the Second World War. At first there were only four questions asked, on housing, families, age and occupation, but subsequently existing questions were varied and new questions were added. It was realised that too many questions might lead to resentment and consequent inaccuracy. Therefore, since 1961 the decennial census has taken a 10 per cent random sample for deeper questioning, while leaving the other 90 per cent to answer the few basic questions on sex, age, marriage, birthplace, citizenship and fertility. An additional 10 per cent sample was taken in a special census in 1966 which did not involve the rest of the population at all.

Looking at a census form. Population censuses are carried out under the terms of the Census Act of 1920. The Registrar General is given power to count the population at intervals of five years, but the convention is that a complete census is held every ten years.

The most essential continuous source of demographic information comes from the registration of births, deaths and marriages, for it is these facts that illustrate the pattern of population change. The church kept incomplete records from medieval times but the state has demanded the information only recently. The first state to enforce registration of births was Sweden in 1748 and other states have followed rather slowly. The system of registration demanded a network of public officials which few states could afford. Moreover, it only became really necessary when it was important to ascertain people's age accurately, for voting or for stopping the use of child labour. It was for these kinds of reason that compulsory registration was introduced in England and Wales in 1836.

Signing the register. All births, deaths and marriages have to be registered with the Registrar. After a marriage, the bride, groom and witnesses sign the register which records names, surnames, occupations and addresses of the married pair together with the names and occupations of their fathers. These records provide useful information for population studies.

In more recent times the United Nations has helped to popularise and regularise registration procedures through the Population Commission Report (1953) and the Demographic Year Book, first published in 1948. The Year Book shows that 30 per cent of countries do not have any effective registration of births and that these are mainly highly-populated states in Asia and Africa. Records of births, deaths and marriages are therefore clearly inaccurate, especially in those areas of the world where population problems are most acute.

MEASURING FERTILITY

The most usual condition of any world population at the present time is one of growth and therefore demographers are predominantly interested in rates of growth and how they can be measured.

One measure of the condition within a community is the *crude birth rate*. This records the number of live births in a year to the total population of all ages. It is expressed as a rate per 1000. This is of very little use in measuring fertility because it gives no heed to the age of the population, the number of marriages that have recently occurred or the balance of the sexes.

More useful is an expression of the number of births as a ratio of the female population who are capable of child-bearing (aged between fifteen and forty-five). This is called the *fertility rate*. It too has shortcomings as it does not properly distinguish the women who are more likely to have children, that is, those who are married. As the vast majority of children are born in marriage and early rather than late in marriage, predictions based on the fertility rate would be very wrong if a threat of war suddenly caused many women to bring forward their wedding day.

The next stage in demographic technique was to take more consideration of the age composition of the female population. Women capable of child-bearing were divided into five-yearly age groups, 15–19, 20–24, 25–29 and so on and the number of children born to the average woman in each group in a year assessed. This would amount to a fraction of a child like 0.1 and it would have to be multiplied by five to give the total likely fertility of a woman in the whole five-year period. The fertility rates for all the age groups are then added together and give the number of children to be expected from the average woman in the course of a life-time.

What the demographer really wants to know is the *replacement rate* of the population, so he is interested in the number of *female* children born to the *average* woman. This is not quite as easy as dividing the number of children by two, as slightly more boys are born than girls, but once the necessary weighting is given, the answer is called the *gross reproduction rate*. This is an expression of the number of female children to be expected from the average woman in a life-time.

A further refinement of this figure is to take into consideration the number of female children born who will survive to child-bearing age themselves. This is called the *net reproduction rate*. It is assessed by multiplying the gross reproduction rate by the survival factor. An example of the mathematics involved is given in the following table:

A large family. This picture of a father and his ten children is large by present-day standards. Families of this size would have been far more common in the nineteenth century.

England and Wales, 1965

Age Group	Fertility rate (female births)	Survival factor	
(1)	(2)	(3)	(2)×(3)
15–19	0·02163	0·9647	0·02087
20–24	0·08565	0·9609	0·08230
25–29	0·08661	0·9559	0·08279
30–34	0·04936	0·9500	0·04689
35–39	0·02365	0·9425	0·02229
40–44	0·00611	0·9321	0·00570
45–49	0·00046	0·9168	0·00042
	0·27347		0·26126

Female gross reproduction rate = 5 × 0·27347 or 1·367
Female net reproduction rate = 5 × 0·26126 or 1·306

These techniques still do not take enough consideration of marriage and demographers are now seeking to build this consideration and others such as the spacing of children into the comparative process. The basic unit of consideration is the family composed of man, woman and children as this is the most nearly universal of all human institutions. Changes in the average size of the family are as accurate a guide to changing population patterns as any.

Demographers can build up their own data on social change by a method called *cohort analysis*. A cohort is a group of people (usually one thousand), born in a particular year or married in a particular year, whose fortunes are monitored. If such samples are taken regularly, the demographer is able to note changes in the favoured age of marriage or in family size.

REPRODUCTIVE CAPACITY

An important consideration in the study of population is the total number of children that a woman is capable of producing. Women are usually able to bear children for about thirty years of their lives, roughly between the ages of fifteen and forty-five. Within these thirty years an average woman could bear between ten and twelve children. This average is dependent on good health and adequate diet and would not be reached by the average woman of a less-advanced country. Throughout most of Asia the average child-bearing period is no more than twenty years and the average family size no more than seven or eight children.

The factors which limit human fruitfulness are many. The first is the rhythm of the woman's body. A woman is fertile for only part of the menstrual cycle of which

(*Opposite*) A child marriage. Marriages are contracted very early in India, often before the couple reach physical maturity. The 1951 Census showed that there were 3 million bridegrooms and 6 million brides between the ages of 5 and 14. This custom contributes to both high fertility and a high death rate amongst both mothers and babies.

there are usually thirteen in a year. There is therefore the probability of a number of unsuccessful attempts to produce a child before conception is achieved. There is then the nine months that the baby is in the womb, which is followed by a further period of infertility usually lasting at least three months after childbirth. This period of infertility will last for much longer if the mother feeds her own child. The body seems to postpone the return of normal fertility while milk is still being taken from the breast.

It is usual for a woman not to conceive a further child for twenty months after the last conception. If it is accepted that ten months is needed for successful conception, taking into account miscarriages as well, then the usual gap between children will be thirty months. Demographers say that if no attempt is made to limit fertility, a married woman is likely to produce one child every two and a half years while she is capable of bearing children. This is not to deny that many children are born at a fourteen-month interval or less, nor that some women bear twenty-five children or more in a life-time. It merely establishes the average fertility of women.

In virtually no community do women produce the maximum number of children of which they are capable. One exception is the Hutterite community in America. It is a rural community of devout Lutherans who practise community of goods and believe it to be a religious duty to bear as many children as possible. The Hutterites marry at the earliest opportunity and produce children steadily. The average Hutterite family has eight children which conforms to expected average total reproductive capacity.

There are many factors which reduce the total reproductive capacity of a community. A number of marriages remain childless. The British Royal Commission on population estimated that 8 per cent of all marriages in Britain were infertile. Even among couples marrying before the age of twenty, 3 per cent were infertile in Britain and just under 3 per cent in South Africa and Vietnam. Among some primitive tribes, infertility in marriage is so high that communities are rapidly dying out. Among the tribesmen of the Andaman Islands the proportion of childless marriages was 45 per cent in 1901 among women who had only had one husband. The reason for this level of infertility in primitive tribes is the prevalence of venereal disease.

Attitudes to marriage also have their effect on the reproductive capacity of women. The proportion of women who become married varies very greatly from continent to continent. Most African women become married, usually at a very early age. Less than 5 per cent of African women remain unmarried and most of them are married before the age of twenty. In case of widowhood African women are likely to be remarried quickly due to the surplus of males and the social encouragement of remarriage. Indian women tend to marry young yet here there is little chance of a second marriage in strict Hindu families. Just over one hundred years ago widows were still burnt on their husband's funeral pyre, but now they are merely forbidden to remarry. Polygamy is practised in some Middle Eastern and North African countries by those who can afford more than one wife. This limits the total reproductive capacity of a woman in the harem as she will be ignored as she becomes older.

Europe has favoured late marriage and also non-marriage. Marriage is usually postponed until after the age of twenty and there is substantial evidence for even later marriage in the sixteenth century which makes it something of a tradition. The practice of late marriage and non-marriage has spread to America and other places where Europeans have migrated and exerted an influence. In Latin America the number of women who never marry is as high as 25 per cent and the number in Europe is 20 per cent.

Man is slow-breeding by the standards of the animal world. Total reproductive capacity is not high even when the population is well fed and in good health. In areas of poor hygiene and deficient diet like most of Africa, the prevailing family size may be as low as four or five. If methods of controlling birth can be spread round the world as successfully as methods of controlling death, sometime in the future world population should reach an equilibrium.

Suttee. This was the Indian custom by which widows burnt themselves on the funeral pyre of their husband with due ceremony. This practice was forbidden by law during the Governor Generalship of Lord William Bentinck (1828-35).

3 CONTROL OF BIRTH AND DEATH RATE

THE TRANSITION THEORY

The rate of growth of a population depends on the rate of natural increase; that is, the difference between the birth rate and the death rate. A balanced population is one which has reached a situation where the number of births exactly balances the number of deaths. Pre-industrial populations had a very slow rate of growth and were sometimes stationary, but this was rarely due to an exact balance of births and deaths.

In precise studies of the population of an English village called Colyton, in Devon, it has been shown that birth rates and death rates kept in balance over very long periods. In the shorter term, baptisms might exceed burials for almost a century, as they did from 1560 to the plague outbreak of 1645; or burials might exceed births over a long period, as they did from 1665 to 1735. At another Devon village called Hartland a smaller crisis shown by a sudden rise in burials seemed to occur every generation, keeping the population in balance. In both villages, a virtually permanent excess of baptisms over burials occurred after 1770 even though they were far from the centres of industrial growth.

The rise in population at the end of the eighteenth century in Colyton coincided with rather earlier marriage which in turn reflected the increasing prosperity of the village. This, repeated over the whole country, could explain the eighteenth-century population rise. There certainly seems no reason to explain it by a decline in the death rate apart from the end of plague catastrophes, for there is no evidence of an appreciable falling off in burials.

Sweden has the most complete set of birth and death records for the eighteenth century and here too there was a slight rise in births before the end of the eighteenth century and a marked decline in the death rate in the mid-eighteenth century. The higher birth rate here is explained by higher fertility in the marriages that took place, for there was a decline in the number who married between 1750 and 1800.

Any increase in family size or bringing forward of marriage seems to have come about as a response to prosperous conditions. The rise in the birth rate can be tentatively attributed to a rising prosperity over all of Western Europe. In the nineteenth century the startling increase in population was almost wholly due to a

The eviction of Irish peasants 1848. The Irish peasantry never had much security in their own land. Their smallholdings were usually rented from English landowners, who had little concern for their poverty. They were particularly vulnerable after the potato famine of 1845. They were therefore strongly attracted by the opportunities for a new life in the United States of America and migrated if they could afford the passage.

decline in the death rate, for as expectation of life increased, so levels of fertility fell. The way in which this occurred in both England and France is illustrated in the diagram.

In the case of both England and France the decline in the death rate was at first rather slow, but there was an acceleration after 1870. The birth rate remained higher than the death rate, but matched its movement downward fairly closely. The English and Welsh pattern is rather closer to the normal experience of states that have undergone the process of industrialisation and it has been explained by what is known as the *transition theory*.

The crude birth rates and death rates in England and France, 1750-1950. Although the figures have been dropping, in England the population is still expanding, whilst France in 1950 had achieved a stable population. (From *The Economic History of World Population*, 1962 edition, Penguin Books.)

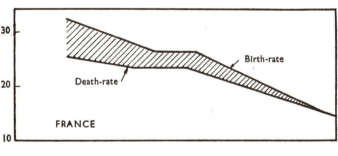

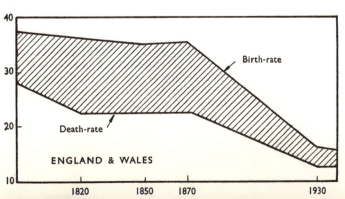

29

This theory seeks to demonstrate how population growth steadies as the level of wealth rises in society. The reason for the decrease in family size as people become more wealthy is connected with the increasing desire of prosperous people to enjoy the attractive goods and opportunities that industry can provide. At the present time many young couples feel that it is important to provide themselves with a house, a car and a television before starting their family. In the nineteenth century parents tried to keep down the size of their family so that they could give their children a good start in life. This might involve an expensive education and help to start the son in his job. So in industrialised countries the rate of population growth is slowed down. There is a *transition* from the rapid growth rate of an agricultural society to the moderate growth rate of an industrial society. The transition theory explains the experience of most advanced nations in recent times, but there are exceptions like France and Ireland.

France's level of fertility has been consistently low in modern history, so much so that at times in the late nineteenth and early twentieth century, birth rates were well below replacement level. The causes of this phenomenon will be examined in Chapter 5.

The case of Ireland was somewhat different. Its population fell from 8·2 million in 1843 to 4·5 million by the end of the century. Prior to the potato famine of 1845, Ireland's population had increased at a phenomenal rate. The population in 1750 had been quite modest at 3·1 million yet it proceeded almost to treble within the next ninety-five years. The increase was associated with the adoption of the potato as the staple food. Potatoes required only a third of the acreage of wheat and could support a large population on a dull diet. The effect of the famine was to persuade many Irish people to emigrate and others to impose their own population checks. The size of Irish families remained high by European standards, but the checks were imposed by late marriage or widespread non-marriage. In 1900 for instance, 59 per cent of Irish women between the ages of twenty-five and twenty-nine were unmarried.

The Irish predicament illustrates the problems of a pre-industrial situation solved partly by the chance of migration to new continents and partly by a fairly disciplined social response to the problem of overpopulation. The Asian states face a similar build-up of pressure on their food resources without the chance of migration into empty spaces enjoyed by the Irish. The increase of Asian, African and Latin American populations is the result of a rapid decline in mortality rates before society was able to adjust the traditional attitudes to age of marriage and control of birth.

According to the transition theory, parents naturally adjust the size of their family downwards when better education, improved health, better-paid jobs, city conditions and higher ambitions for their children show them the benefit of having a smaller number of children. The underdeveloped countries have not been able to provide these benefits for enough of their population for any transition to occur Other means will therefore have to be found to control population until the transition has been achieved.

BIRTH CONTROL

Few societies have made women bear children to their full reproductive capacity. There is plenty of evidence for the restraint of fertility in pre-industrial society merely by the postponement of marriage or by the limitation of births within marriage. Poor peasant families have had no artificial devices to help them except for noxious brews suggested in the folk lore of various civilisations, which were probably ineffective. For instance, a recipe reported recently from China recommended the swallowing of twenty-four tadpoles a few days after menstruation. Yet there is evidence where statistics exist, as at Colyton in Devon, that family limitation was achieved. How they achieved it is a matter for conjecture.

Artificial methods of contraception seem to have been used quite successfully in France in the seventeenth and eighteenth centuries involving the use of a vaginal sponge and this early experience of family limitation may have some bearing on the slowness of French population growth subsequently. Yet demographers are very reluctant to explain declines in population in these terms, for family limitation is practised for social and economic reasons and it is only in recent years that birth control has been practised by the majority of families in any community.

One of the most popular devices from the nineteenth century onwards was the condom or male sheath. It was named after a seventeenth-century English doctor, but it did not became widely available until the invention of vulcanised rubber. A female equivalent in the form of a diaphragm device closing the vaginal passage was invented by a German doctor in 1880. The efficiency of these methods was improved further by the provision of spermicidal creams in the twentieth century. There was considerable opposition within society, directed by the churches, to these methods. Intrepid supporters of birth control methods like Annie Besant and Charles Bradlaugh were virtually ostracised by society. Great publicity was given to their campaign for the spreading of knowledge in birth control methods by their trial, suspended prison sentence and subsequent acquittal on appeal in 1877 and 1878. Around a million tracts giving contraceptive advice were sold in England between 1876 and 1891.

In the early twentieth century the whole subject of birth control became respectable as people came to accept it not as the road to promiscuity but as a recipe for happy families. Marie Stopes did much work in the development of clinics where education

Charles Bradlaugh (1833–1891). He and Annie Besant were early supporters of birth control in Britain. They were both brought to trial in 1876 for publishing a pamphlet advocating birth control and it was this that brought the subject to the public notice. They were sentenced to six months' imprisonment and a £200 fine but this conviction was quashed on appeal.

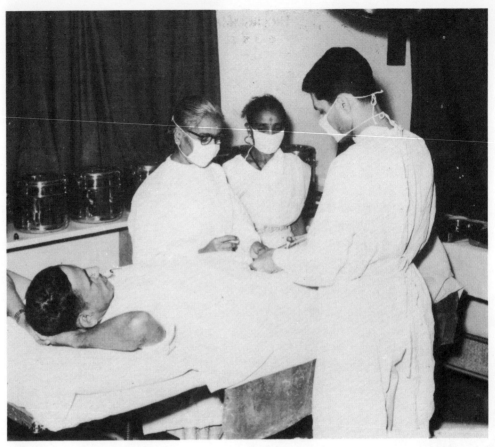

Vasectomy (male sterilization) operation in progress. This is a relatively simple piece of surgery and does not involve keeping the patient in hospital. Indian men have been encouraged to undergo the operation by government propaganda and by the offer of prizes.

in the use of birth control methods could be given. Her attitude was summarised in a speech she made soon after the opening of the first birth control clinic in the British Empire in 1921. 'It is extraordinary how the words "birth control" have become associated with a negative and repressive movement. . . . By birth control I mean not merely the repression of lives which ought not be be started, but the bringing into the world of healthy, happy, desired babies.' This aspect was emphasised when the National Birth Control Association changed its name to the Family Planning Association in 1939.

Birth control was accepted by the Church of England at the Lambeth Conference of 1930 'in those cases where there was a clearly-felt moral obligation to limit or avoid parenthood, and where there was a morally sound reason for avoiding complete abstinence' but the Roman Catholic Church still opposes it except by natural methods. Family planning by moral restraint and by 'proper' use of the rhythm method was recognised; this means that Catholics are required to utilise the time of woman's natural infertility, or the so-called 'safe period', if they wish to avoid births.

Much knowledge and advice has been available to married couples in the Western world in recent years and it is probable that most people in the West consciously limit conception at some time in their married lives. Precise statistics on these matters are not available as the questions involved are so personal and delicate, but sample studies suggest that although contraception is widely practised, people are not as sophisticated as is sometimes presumed.

More recent contraceptive practice has favoured methods that do not intrude on the act of love-making. The Pill is now widely used by women to suppress ovulation. It is not perfect as it has to be taken everyday according to a prescribed pattern and for some women it has side effects. A more final method is to be sterilised and this is quite widely accepted as a solution by both men and women.

The male operation is called vasectomy and is relatively simple. It can also, in some circumstances, be reversed. As it does not demand complex hospital facilities, it is one of the most favoured forms of birth control in India. Another favoured method of birth control in underdeveloped countries is the IUD (intra-uterine device) which is also known as the coil or loop. This involves the semi-permanent insertion of a small device into the womb. The loop has the effect of stopping the implantation of the egg on the wall of the womb and while it remains in place it is effective. It does not involve peasant women in difficult procedures needing hygienic surroundings and is quite acceptable to most Asian populations.

All the methods considered so far stop the process of conception, but it is also possible to kill the foetus or the infant. The killing of the foetus is called abortion and is becoming more and more acceptable in advanced societies. Abortion is not available on demand in England but it can be carried out on the advice of two doctors where it is for the benefit of the mother and her existing family. Abortion by legal means is rather easier to secure in Eastern Europe and in Hungary it has been more common than live birth in the last decade. The birth rate in some Eastern European countries has been uniformly low in recent years and easily available abortion seems to be the cause. Robert McNamara, commenting on the prevalence of illegal abortion in 1969, said, 'Statistics suggest that abortion is one of the world's commonest methods to limit fertility – despite the fact that in most societies it is ethically offensive, illegal, expensive and medically hazardous'.

Birth control in all its forms is surrounded by moral problems but as the years pass the virtues of stopping unwanted children are stronger in people's minds than the evils of stopping life. It really seems to be a case of making a virtue of necessity.

DEATH CONTROL

There was no startling improvement in life expectation until after 1870 which is well after the beginning of industrial change. The reason for this is that the conditions in the new industrial areas did not make it easy to keep healthy. For a long time there was a much better chance of living a long life in the countryside than in the towns. It was not until the middle of the nineteenth century that the Earl of

Shaftesbury's campaign for factory reform and Edwin Chadwick's for uniform standards of public health, resulted in effective parliamentary legislation to cope with exploitation in the factories and filth in the towns in England. Around the same time other countries in Northern, Western and Central Europe and the overseas countries colonised by them were legislating to improve standards of housing, water supply and cleanliness in towns. It was the improvement of the physical surroundings in towns and cities that suppressed many of the diseases such as typhoid, scarlet fever, diphtheria and tuberculosis that had weakened city people.

Apart from plague, which became less common in the eighteenth century with the replacement of the black rat by the grey, the main killer was smallpox. This disease was brought under control by the discovery by Edward Jenner in 1796 that the body built up a resistance to the disease if the patient was infected with a dose of the milder complaint called cowpox. Louis Pasteur later discovered the nature of the bacteria that caused many diseases and around 1879 began the process of finding vaccines. So began the modern practice of immunisation which soon covered diseases like cholera, typhoid, plague, yellow fever and typhus.

Hospitals were greatly improved at the end of the nineteenth century, practising the devoted methods of modern nursing established by Florence Nightingale during the Crimean War, 1854–56. Pain was eliminated from the operating theatre by the discovery and acceptance of anaesthetics around 1850. Most important of all, Joseph Lister, working from the logic of Pasteur's work on micro-organisms, began to use antiseptics in the operating theatre after 1870. Many factors were therefore working to save lives that might otherwise have been lost through infection and disease and together they account for the rapid fall in mortality which was sustained into the twentieth century.

The highest mortality has always occurred at birth and it was the newly-born babies who were particularly vulnerable in the dirty, industrial towns. Infant death rates per 1000 live births was still 157 in England and Wales in the period 1864–70 but had fallen to 72 by 1921–30. Figures that are worse than these still prevail in many underdeveloped countries. North West Nigeria showed an infant mortality rate of 294 per 1000 in 1948. The level of the death rate in early life is a crucial test of the health services and the general social progress of the country in question.

There has been further progress in the control of death in recent years. Antibiotics have helped further in the control of infection and vaccines have been found for most of the killer diseases, the most recent being the BCG vaccine against tuberculosis and the Salk vaccine for poliomyelitis. In the advanced parts of the world most people can expect to live until the age of seventy and the infant death rate has been cut down to between twenty and fifty for every 1,000 live births. The lower figure prevails in America, England, Sweden, Australia and New Zealand.

The techniques for controlling disease have taken about 200 years to perfect, yet this accumulated wisdom is available to underdeveloped countries all at once. The World Health Organisation, an agency of the United Nations, helps to spread the knowledge and also plans international attacks on the diseases common to these

(*Opposite*) Water-supply in Calcutta. Many inhabitants of Calcutta have to depend on water supply from pipes like this. The supply is short, so people tend to use any water that is available, which results in a harvest of water-borne diseases.

areas like malaria, yaws and leprosy. Spraying policies have brought many of the insect-borne diseases under control very quickly. The death rate among babies in Georgetown, Guyana, dropped from 250 per thousand to 67 per thousand after DDT had been sprayed over a ten square mile (twenty-six square kilometre) area round and including the city, between 1945 and 1948. Dramatic falls in deaths from malaria have occurred quite suddenly as a result of world-wide spraying of the swamps where the anopheles mosquito breeds. In Mauritius for instance, life expectation at birth increased from thirty-three years in 1946 to fifty-one years in 1953 after the eradication of malaria. The effect of such a sudden population rise to an island economy with a tradition of high fertility could be quite alarming. In Mauritius however, the population has responded very quickly to the inherent danger and the birth rate dropped from 40 births per 1,000 people in 1963 to 30 births per 1,000 in 1967.

(*Above*) Locust protection. The desert locust is capable of destroying crops in a very short time. Swarms of them plague many countries from West Africa to India. Once the locusts take to the air in their millions they are impossible to contain. The best chance to control them occurs when the locusts are still confined to the ground in the 'hopper' stage. Many countries in East Africa co-operate to carry out aerial spraying programmes helped by the Food and Agricultural Organisation (FAO) of the United Nations.

(*Opposite*) The World Health Organisation (WHO) in Ethiopia. This doctor in Ethiopia is primarily concerned with investigating health to discover from which diseases Ethiopians suffer and die. The results of the survey will enable the Ethiopian Government to organise health services better. The child with a bandaged head is suffering from scabies.

Mortality will drop still further in some areas of the world like Tropical and West Africa, but in many others life expectancy is approaching that of the Western world and infant mortality is low. Man has gained momentary control over death and can maintain it with continued vigilance. The change from high mortality to low mortality has been so sudden that most governments and populations are only just assimilating the full meaning of this change. Islands like Mauritius have had to react quickly: other areas of the world like Africa and South America are still relatively under-populated and can afford to react much more slowly.

FAMILY SIZE
The family is still the most widely accepted institution in the world. In the more primitive areas the family is often seen as the extended family or kinship group, including at least three generations of grandparents, parents and children and other relatives as well. In these family groups the burden of extra children is not felt so greatly by the parents as the children will be brought up by the whole family group, the grandparents in particular. New births are a source of joy to the whole lineage in some tribes such as the Ashanti in Ghana as it increases its collective power and prestige. In societies where the family is the conjugal group of father, mother and children, the nuclear family, there is often a desire for many sons as a guarantee of a male heir. Moreover a large family gives a better chance of help and support to the parents in old age. For these reasons there was no fear of large families in most parts of the world while mortality was high.

The development of the family in the Western world has been towards a family of two or three. The lowest point of family size in recent years was reached in the two decades after the First World War when the average size so nearly approached two that demographers thought that the population of many important industrialised nations, including Great Britain, would soon begin to fall. There was a recovery during and after the Second World War which has kept the population steadily rising.

The smaller family began to become fashionable during the latter half of the nineteenth century. Victorian families amongst both lower and middle classes were well known for their size. The average family size before 1870 seems to have been about six. The lower classes are thought to have reared children quite freely in the new towns as there were so many opportunities for child labour until the middle of the century, while middle-class homes were large, comfortable and well supplied with servants. The decline set in first for middle-class families. The reason for the decline seems connected with growing middle-class expectations.

A period of prosperity up to 1870 gave the upper and middle classes a taste for comfort and the fruits of wealth, but the harder times after that date led to a need for economies and a reduction of family size. The growing educational and career

opportunities meant that there was much to be gained from expensive education and by the end of the century this was being provided by fee-paying schools for both boys and girls. Middle-class families could only afford this type of education for a small family. After 1870, state education began to be provided and it soon became compulsory. This meant that children could no longer be expected to pay their way quickly and even the working class had to consider how many dependent children they could afford.

In the twentieth century the trend towards smaller families became more pronounced. The First World War broke down many of the prejudices against working wives and the campaign for the emancipation of women made wives question their duty to bear and rear large families. Another powerful force in the contraction of family size was the atmosphere of pessimism after the Great War. There had been so much suffering and loss of life in the 1914–18 War that many felt that the world was not a fit place for the rearing of children; others were put off by the shortage of jobs once the post-war depression began in 1920. The experience of depression and unemployment in particular led to a fall in fertility in the working classes, bringing them more into line with the family size of the richer classes, which had begun to fall earlier. This population pattern was apparent in almost all the advanced industrialised countries; only Eastern and Southern Europe still showed a high birth rate during the inter-war years.

There has been a slight recovery of fertility since the Second World War and the size of the average family has moved nearer to three than two. This increase was

Harrow School. The desire of middle-class parents to provide their children with a good start in life led them to limit the size of their families to the number that they could expensively educate. This motive still operates today, even though State secondary education is provided for all.

particularly marked in the period 1955–65 and seemed connected with the affluence of the post-war recovery and the attendant high employment. Another factor was the tendency for more people to marry and to marry earlier. This also seems to be connected with levels of employment and the real income of the younger age group. The new generation of married people of all classes seemed well versed in birth control techniques and were able to confine their family-making to a period of six to eight years, after which the wife often prepared to return to her former career.

Comfortable homes. In the twentieth century it has been increasingly tempting to spend available money on the provision of comfortable and well-equipped homes. As domestic help has become very expensive, much attention has been devoted to providing elegant labour-saving kitchens. Family-making is delayed or curtailed while such homes are financed.

The link between size of family and occupation has been a factor of great interest to demographers. The greater the ambition of the parents to rise in society, the smaller the size of the family was likely to be. Those who had little opportunity of rising in the social scale, like labourers or peasants, had no reason to constrain their reproductive habits and had larger families than anyone else. Those, on the other hand, who wanted all the trappings of wealth in the form of fine housing, lavish fixtures and expensive education for their children would limit their family size.

This theory seemed to incorporate most of the data until the end of the Second World War. Professional and managerial families were almost always smaller than the families of unskilled factory workers and farm labourers. In underdeveloped countries it was graduates and professional people whose family size began to decline first, whereas the families of peasants and miners remained at the traditionally high level. In fact, in places like Formosa, Puerto Rico and Egypt that enjoy quite sophisticated educational systems, it is possible to demonstrate a link between education and fertility. As recently as 1960 the average size of family for illiterates in Egypt was seven or eight, for secondary school leavers, three or four and for college leavers two or three.

What has happened since the Second World War in the developed areas is that the family size at the lower end of the social scale has continued to fall while the families of the professional classes have risen slightly. Social differences in family size have therefore been ironed out to a great extent. From an educational point of view, fertility tables produced from the English 1961 census data showed that there was still a relatively high fertility rate for those with a modest degree of education and a declining fertility rate as educational level increased, until the university and college level where there was an increase in relative fertility. There is a similar growth of family size within the better educated groups of professional or managerial people in the United States of America.

Family size for white wives in the USA aged 35–39 by occupation of their husband in 1940, 1950 and 1960

	1940	1950	1960
Farm labourers and foremen	3·6	3·7	4·0
Farmers	3·5	3·3	3·2
Labourers	3·0	2·9	3·0
Craftsmen and foremen	2·4	2·2	2·7
Clerical staff and salesmen	1·7	1·8	2·4
Managers	1·9	2·0	2·5
Professional and technical	1·7	1·8	2·5

New theories are now being propounded that family size is an expression of wealth in the affluent societies of the Western world and that it will be the richer classes that feel able to afford a third and a fourth child. Before the Industrial

Old People's Home. Such homes are becoming more and more common as the percentage of old people in the British population increases. As population becomes more mobile and homes become smaller, it is increasingly difficult for people to depend on their own families in old age.

Revolution it was the wealthier and better-educated families which had more children and it may be that industrialisation has only temporarily reversed the situation in favour of the poorer classes.

AGE STRUCTURE

The distribution of age groups within a population is a very important consideration. Only part of any population is productive and on these working adults falls the responsibility of maintaining both the young and old. Any great increase in the proportion of the young or the old to the working force will mean that more dependents will have to be supported by fewer productive workers. This in turn could put a strain on the whole community.

Most developed countries are ageing in this sense. The percentage of people aged over sixty in a pre-industrial community or in a community with a continuing high mortality rate would be 6 or 7 per cent. This was the figure in Egypt in 1950 and Russia in 1939. In nations like France, Sweden, Great Britain and Germany in 1961 the figure was 17 per cent. In all of these nations even though each generation is slightly larger than the last, the proportion of old people continues to rise. It has been estimated that if people continue to die at the same average age as they do today, and the population remains stationary, there would be 24 per cent of people over sixty.

The explanation of this ageing phenomenon is not the lower mortality rates, for the decrease of infant mortality increases the size of the generation at the lower end of the age structure at the same time as it increases life expectation at the upper end. The main factor in ageing is decreasing fertility and this has already been demonstrated in the developed world.

The situation in underdeveloped countries is the exact reverse. An improvement in mortality rates usually reflects a dramatic decline in infant deaths and if fertility rates remain high as well, this means that the young generations become larger in relation to the older ones. Many countries in South America, Africa and Asia are moving into this phase of falling mortality and high fertility and in the process the population is becoming younger. This brings its own difficulties as more children mean that more schools will have to be provided to educate them and eventually more jobs will have to be found for them to do.

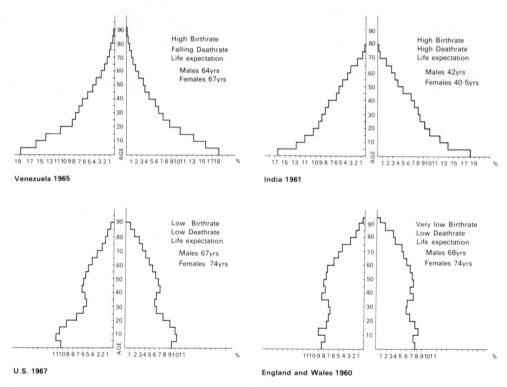

Venezuela 1965

High Birthrate
Falling Deathrate
Life expectation
Males 64yrs
Females 67yrs

India 1961

High Birthrate
High Deathrate
Life expectation
Males 42yrs
Females 40·5yrs

U.S. 1967

Low Birthrate
Low Deathrate
Life expectation
Males 67yrs
Females 74yrs

England and Wales 1960

Very low Birthrate
Low Deathrate
Life expectation
Males 68yrs
Females 74yrs

These pyramids enable comparison between the age-grouping of different populations. The left-hand side of each diagram shows the males; the right-hand side the females. It can be seen that in Venezuela and India the population is relatively young. The birth rate is high, but not many children live to adulthood. In America and Britain the age groups are more evenly distributed. Great wars and depressions account for the smaller numbers in the young adult age groups between the ages of twenty and thirty-five. (Sources of statistics on which these diagrams are based are as follows: USA and Venezuela, *Population – Facts and Methods of Demography*, 1971, by Nathan Keyfitz and Wilhelm Flieger, W. H. Freeman and Co. California; India and England and Wales, *The Growth and Control of World Population* by W. D. Borries, Weidenfeld and Nicolson Ltd, London.)

The different age structures can be illustrated in diagrammatic form in population pyramids. These show India as a balanced population where the generations become uniformly smaller as they rise in age. Although it makes the neatest pyramid, it is not in the happiest position, as the precision of the pyramid steps is only the result of uniformly high mortality. An even less happy age structure would be one that is fatter in the middle than it is at the bottom. England and Wales have avoided this, but not by much.

BALANCE OF THE SEXES

It is an interesting fact that more males are born than females in the ratio of about 105 males to 100 females. Moreover, there is a tendency for the males ratio to increase in time of war and this has led to speculation on the 'hidden hand' that compensates for male losses during war. The phenomenon can be explained however, by the higher proportion of male children among first births. War tends to accelerate marriage and there tends to be more first births in war-time then in peace-time.

Despite the fact that males are usually bigger and stronger at birth, females have tended to outnumber males in the population as a whole. They live longer and are not so liable to the hazards of life as the male. In Britain the life expectation of a male is sixty-nine years and of a female seventy-five years, so it is probable that women stand up better to the rigours of life in other ways as well. In the lower age groups males are beginning to outnumber females, but predictions from the 1971 United Kingdom population census suggest that by 2011 males will still only comprise 49·4 per cent of the population compared with 48·6 per cent in 1971.

Females do not show this predominance everywhere. In India, for instance, there is a curious deficiency of women. This appears to be the result of the greater value that parents put upon boys, with the result that the girls are relatively neglected in childhood. Indian females remain at a disadvantage throughout their lives and this is expressed in the most unusual fact that the Indian male can expect to live for forty-six years while the Indian woman has a life expectation of only forty-four years. A similar situation prevails in Pakistan, but everywhere else the woman lives longer.

MIGRATION

The inflow and outflow of people from one country to another is also an important factor in population. Historically there have been vast movements of peoples which have changed the racial character of whole regions. The movement of negro slaves from Africa to the American continent from the sixteenth century onwards has had an enormous effect on the population of the Caribbean and the Southern States of America. As the slave trade was finishing, the movement of white Europeans to America, Canada, Australia and New Zealand became the great migratory movement. It was the countries of Northern and Western Europe, particularly Great Britain, which contributed to this flow up to the First World War. When the Great War finished it was Southern and Eastern Europe, where the birth rate continued at a

West Indians in London. West Indians began to migrate to Britain in substantial numbers in the 1950s. There were few jobs for them in their home islands and it became clear that those who went to Britain found work quite easily. By 1961 there were 172,379 residents of Britain who were born in the British West Indies. Controls were imposed by the Commonwealth Immigration Act, 1962 and since then the flow has lessened. The West Indians are English-speaking and often pride themselves on their smartness.

high level, which supplied the largest number of emigrants. During the period 1846–1939 some fifty-one million people left Europe. Of these, thirty-eight million went to the USA, seven million to Canada, seven million to Argentina, and two and a half million to Australia.

The USA continued to be the greatest receiver of immigrants after the Second World War. For a time after the 1914–18 War, American industry was so depressed that it could not absorb immigrant labour as readily as before, and restrictions were imposed by the US Quota Acts of 1921 and the Immigration Restriction Act of 1924. Since 1945 however, the USA has absorbed a further 4·3 million immigrants, just over half of them from Europe. Great as the flow was, it still only contributed a fraction of the population increase of just under three million each year.

The decline of the birth rate in the countries of Northern, Western and Central Europe, which reached a low point in the two decades between the World Wars, meant that there was only a slow increase in the work force in this area after 1945. Although there was no hindrance to emigration (and positive encouragement from the government of the Netherlands), the rate began to decrease considerably. The demand for labour in what was still one of the most important industrial areas in the world had to be fed from elsewhere to compensate. West Germany, which rapidly recovered from the effect of war, was fed in turn by repatriated Germans and a growing flow of refugees from East Germany. Once the Common Market was formed

Southern Italians migrating north. This has been a familiar direction of migration since the Second World War. Southern Italy can provide little work for growing peasant families and the men therefore have to move into the industrial areas of northern Italy and the Common Market to find work.

in 1957, a free market in labour was opened within the six countries which allowed Italians to move northwards even more freely.

Unlike Northern and Central Europe, Southern Europe had a high birth rate between the wars and this provided a large young working population after the Second World War. This was particularly true of Italy, which had light war casualties and a low rate of industrial investment. Between 1946 and 1960 there was a flow of just under two million Italians to the main immigrant countries outside Europe but since then Italy has been able to absorb its potential work force much better. Spain, Portugal and Greece have been displaying similar migratory patterns.

The United Kingdom has attracted a considerable immigrant population since 1945. There was no surplus working population after the Second World War, yet the movement to the USA, Australia, Canada and New Zealand continued. There was a great demand for labour to do the less-attractive and badly-paid jobs and this was fed by Commonwealth immigrants from the West Indies and from India and Pakistan. The numbers that had arrived from non-white areas was estimated to be just under 500,000 in 1965.

By this time, Britain had given up its traditional role as a net exporter of people and now received more people from abroad than it lost by emigration. The danger signals now went up that Britain might be swamped by the faster-increasing immigrant people. Strict curbs were therefore put on Commonwealth immigrants in 1962. They would not be given entry vouchers unless they had a specific job to go to or a particular skill which was required in the United Kingdom. There would, however, be no restriction on the dependents of those already in England. By this system of control, Commonwealth immigration has been kept down to a trickle.

Migration is not such an important factor in Asia and Africa. Asians have been positively discouraged from migrating to other continents except on a temporary basis. Small numbers went to Africa to work and this accounts for the small populations of Asians in some African countries. What movement there has been in Asia tends to be from one Asian country to another like the considerable Chinese migration into Singapore and Malaya in the nineteenth century. There was also considerable migration of peoples into India and Pakistan when the Indian sub-continent was divided in 1947.

African migration tends to be of a more temporary kind as it often involves the migration of the male only, while the wife and children remain in their tribal area. Labour in Africa is naturally attracted to the industrial areas of Southern Africa but wages are not high enough to support a man and his family. The husband therefore works for the luxuries while the wife and children continue to live in their agricultural community. The main movement has been from Central and Eastern Africa southwards into South Africa and Southern Rhodesia. It is estimated that some 112,000 Africans migrated into the Union (now the Republic) of South Africa in the late 1950s and of these 75,000 later returned.

The migration movements are becoming much more complex and much more difficult to describe in the absence of accurate census material in many countries.

Multi-racial community. This is the orchestra of a London Comprehensive School. There are a number of second generation immigrants in the picture but as they are dressed in school uniform and share in a common activity, they blend very happily.

It is virtually impossible to distinguish between a migrant and a long-term visitor even in an advanced country. It is only possible to guess what is happening in many Asian and African territories. The chances of populations moving around as pressure on resources in their own country increases are lessening as more and more nations raise barriers against immigration. Movement into developing countries may become increasingly of a temporary nature, for higher education or for the practice of skills in short supply. The nations of the underdeveloped world, facing sudden increases in population, will have to solve their problems within their own frontiers by raising the rate of economic growth.

5 CASE STUDIES

THE UNITED KINGDOM—AN AGEING POPULATION

The population of the United Kingdom in the 1971 census was 55,700,000. This is an increase of three million since the previous census in 1961, when the total was 52,685,000, and suggests a very rapid population increase. It gives a false impression of youth and virility in the British population as a whole, for Britain's population is clearly ageing. The large generations of the 1900s have been replaced by generations which were and still are smaller and in the 1970s these large generations provide a sizeable generation of old age pensioners.

The Royal Commission on Population of 1949 forecast that the British population would reach a plateau in the 1970s and then begin to decrease gradually. This conclusion was reached by projecting forwards the fertility patterns of the 1920s and 30s and taking a special family census in 1946. As far as the Commission's Report was concerned, birth control had been too successful. The results of such rapid ageing of the population were undesirable in the extreme – a declining work force, decreasing demand and a growing percentage of old people. It was suggested that every effort should be made to redress the financial disadvantage of large families and to discourage emigration.

The whole tone of this Commission's Report seems entirely fatuous in the light of the British population recovery since the war. The most generally expressed opinion in the 1970s is that Britain is overpopulated and that the continuing increase is a matter for serious concern. Suggestions are made that large families should be positively discouraged and there are organisations whose members pledge not to have more than two children. The climate of opinion is greatly affected by arguments of ecologists that human pressure on the environment is changing the delicate balances of nature. There are signs that these arguments may be leading to a cut-back in fertility as disturbing as that of the 1920s and 1930s.

The large increase in population between 1961 and 1971 was a reflection of the increasing birth rate of the years 1956 to 1964, when every year showed a substantially greater number of births than the preceding one. Already the 'bulge' of 1946 and 1947 had given a great boost to the population, as families delayed by the war were

(*Opposite*) The hungry thirties. The birth rate fell below replacement level in the 1920s and 1930s. Unemployment was continuously high and many men found it difficult to scratch a living. These men from Pontypridd in South Wales are tending allotments hewn from the hillside and producing some worthwhile crops (1934).

begun or increased, but this was followed by a decline to a level somewhat above that of the pre-war years yet big enough to dispel the fears of an actual decline in population. None of this gave any inkling of the buoyant birth rate of 1956–64 which was to cause demographers to reassess the situation completely. The birth rate in 1964 was over 30 per cent higher than that of 1955, so there were clearly some new factors at play.

One explanation was that a much larger percentage of women were becoming married than before and at a rather earlier age. The Registrar General pointed out that 'marriage rates have been very high, and for the average spinster marriage prospects are about as high as they can be'. Over 80 per cent of women in the twenty to thirty-nine age group were married at the time of the 1961 census. The net reproduction rate was also increasing, indicating a move towards larger families. Other factors at work were an increase in the number of illegitimate births and the great number of Commonwealth immigrants coming from areas of higher fertility. It has been estimated that up to one-third of the additional births of these years could be attributed to the Commonwealth immigrant factor.

The trend of population since 1966 has been tested by the 1971 census and this suggests that the birth rate has steadied once again. The prediction is that the women who married in the late 1960s will have slightly smaller families than those married around 1960. At the same time the legalisation of abortion has decreased the

Welfare State hospital. This kind of hospital service is available to every British citizen under the National Health Scheme. Treatment, nursing and hygiene are so good that most people survive their illnesses. Most advanced countries have comparable hospital services, but few are free under national insurance schemes.

illegitimacy rate; also the flow of Commonwealth immigrants into the country has slowed down greatly. It is thought that the British population will increase by two million by 1981 and at a similar rate into the future. What is clear is that British families react sensitively to the prevailing economic climate and family size becomes a token of their confidence in the future.

Indexes of the trend of fertility in England and Wales and Scotland since 1901

	Average annual crude birth rate per thousand population		Average annual number of legitimate births per thousand married women aged 15–45	Approximate average women's reproduction rate	
	England and Wales	Scotland	England and Wales	England and Wales	
				Gross	Net
1901–5	28·2	29·2	230·5	1·70	1·25
1906–10	26·3	27·6	212·9	1·60	1·20
1911–15	23·6	25·4	190·7	1·45	1·15
1916–20	20·1	22·8	157·0	1·35	1·10
1921–5	19·9	23·0	156·7	1·30	1·10
1926–30	16·7	20·0	130·9	1·10	0·95
1931–5	15·0	18·2	115·2	0·87	0·78
1936–40	14·7	17·6	107·3	0·87	0·79
1941–5	15·9	17·8	105·4	0·96	0·88
1946–50	18·0	20·0	122·5	1·15	1·11
1951–5	15·3	17·9	105·0	1·05	1·02
1956–60	16·4	19·2	113·5	1·20	1·16
1961–5	18·1	19·7	125·9	1·40	1·36
1966–70	17·6	18·4	123·5	1·32	1·28

FRANCE—A SPECIAL CASE

France did not experience a rapid population expansion in the nineteenth century and it is this fact that makes it a special case. The British population has increased ten times since 1700 and the American twenty times since 1820. France today has a population which is only twice as large as it was in 1700. At the time when German population was increasing at a very rapid rate at the end of the nineteenth century, the French population was virtually stationary. The French suffered very heavy losses of life during the First World War. Landry, a French demographer, has estimated that the increase of 14 million in the French population between 1801 and 1936 can be attributed to these gains and losses:

Immigrants and their children	+ 5·5 million
Declining mortality	+16·8 million
War losses in First World War	− 3·0 million

The result of this calculation is a net gain of 19·3 million, which means that there was a serious failure of French reproduction to the tune of 5·3 millions. During these years it was not unusual for deaths to exceed births and most French people seemed content with families of one or two children.

The general effect of France's position in comparison with her neighbours was one of real decline. In 1750 France comprised 15 per cent of Europe's population and in 1939 only 7·9. There seemed to be no bonus in the form of greater capital investment, greater savings or finer living conditions. The only change, in the opinion of Alfred Sauvy, Director of the French National Institute for Demographic Studies, was towards greater indulgence. 'Wine changed from an economic luxury into a tyrant' and the French developed a taste for meat. Life was good, but for lack of stimulating pressure, the building trade became atrophied, the navy stagnated and the colonies declined.

The First World War. All the countries that took part in this war suffered very heavy casualties. Britain lost 750,000 men, France well over a million, Germany about 2 million, Austro-Hungary a million and Russia perhaps 3 million. The battle line was very static on the Western Front and everything in range of the line tended to be bombarded to the ground. This is the city of Cambrai when it was recaptured by the allies in October 1918.

Booming Paris. The Paris area has been one of the major growth areas in Europe since the Second World War. It has attracted population towards the city to find work in factories alongside the river Seine, shown here.

The reasons for this failure of fertility have been the source of much speculation. Much emphasis has been placed on the laws of inheritance in Napoleon's Civil Code which decreed that estates should be divided among the sons. To keep estates from being broken up, families tried to limit male births and thus all births. A more likely reason is the lack of any dynamic phase of technical innovation in France during the nineteenth century, which meant that few centres of economic growth developed in the provinces outside Paris. While the economy and outlook of most French people remained agricultural, they displayed the same deliberate care in their family-making as English pre-industrial communities such as Colyton. If land and housing were not available they delayed marriage.

The French government were so worried by the weakness of the French population after the First World War that the sale of contraceptives was forbidden and measures were taken to provide child allowances, yet the real turning point in French population was delayed until 1939, just before the Second World War. It was then that the *Code de la Famille* was published. As Sauvy remarked, 'The most aged population on earth took, at the most unlikely moment, steps towards a renewal which no other country in the world yet had the courage to imagine'.

After the war, in 1945, the practice of granting allowances was developed into a large and costly social security system aimed to encourage larger families. Already the birth rate had increased during the war, perhaps as an expression of the feeling that in the hour of France's humiliation, procreation was a moral duty, but it rose to a very healthy level after the war. Although the birth rate is now slowly declining again, the French population is now increasing faster than the British. French families have been slightly larger since the war and the number of immigrants also has been slightly higher. French population is now larger than that of England and Wales, but France remains underpopulated by the standards of Western Europe.

AUSTRALIA—A NEW COUNTRY

White settlement of Australia began as recently as 1789, so it can be called a new country despite its long occupation by the aborigines. It depended on immigration for its original growth and its ready welcome of white settlers has now become a national tradition. The rate of immigration has fluctuated enormously from boom periods like the 1850s goldrush to periods of virtual standstill, as is shown by the following table showing net immigration per 1,000 annually of existing population.

1860–69	13·1	1910–13	14·3
1870–79	9·6	1920–29	6·0
1880–89	14·9	1930–38	0·0
1890–99	0·2	1947–51	11·6
1900–09	0·0	1952–60	8·2

Immigration has made a substantial but not a crucial contribution to Australian population growth. During the period 1861–1900, 71 per cent of the increased

Sydney, Australia. Most Australians live in large cities, which are among the most advanced in the world. This is North Sydney, a new growth point on the north side of the famous Sydney Bridge. The new Opera House can be seen just to the left of the bridge.

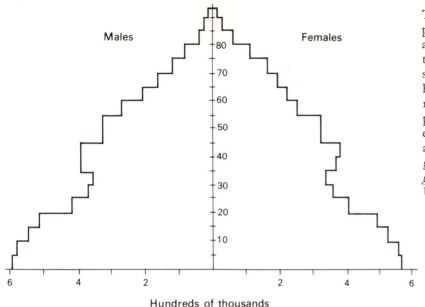

Males   Females

80
70
60
50
40
30
20
10

6   4   2   2   4   6

Hundreds of thousands

The structure of the Australian population in 1966. The central axis shows the age of the population, the base axis shows the size. Australia has a moderately high birth rate and a low death rate. The proportion of young people also reflects to some extent the fact that Australia attracts young immigrants. (Diagram based on figures in *Demography* by Peter Cox, Cambridge University Press, London.)

population was born in Australia and a similar contribution has been made by natural increase towards the recent growth of the Australian population to eleven and a half million. Immigration for permanent settlement is almost entirely confined to Europeans as there has always been a fear in Australia of Asian expansion southwards into the open space of the vast subcontinent of Australia.

The government for a long time has been prepared to offer state-assisted passages for suitable European settlers. Such help was almost wholly confined to British subjects before 1946, but since then equal help has been offered to other Europeans. The demand for labour was such after the Second World War that Australia welcomed a much larger number of refugees than she had first intended; 182,000 entered Australia between 1949 and 1951, for instance. Immigration has progressed steadily since then so that over two million immigrants have settled in Australia since 1945. One million entered on assisted passages and a million were unassisted: about half were British and half non-British. Many of the unassisted European settlers were Italians and Greeks who had very few job opportunities in their own countries after the war.

The age structure of Australia reveals a very well-balanced population with a small percentage of old people. The effect of immigration policy is to keep the average age down, for the aim is to attract young married couples with their families. This means that there is an inflow of people into all generations in the lower age group.

The movement of birth and death rates in Australia has been very similar to that of any other advanced country. Average family size has remained a little above that of Great Britain, but not greatly so. Birth control was practised in Australia by the end of the nineteenth century and was stopping the rapid population increase that

Australian outback. Australia is a vast, open, underpopulated continent, which is too hot and dry for immediate development. Windmills are used to draw water from the natural underground storage reservoirs and this increases the area of pastoral farming.

the state authorities desired. A Royal Commission was appointed by the government of New South Wales to study the decline in the birth rate in 1904 and they reported 'The practices involved in the limitation of families are responsible for much physical suffering, for a deadening of moral sensibility and for degradation of character among those who resort to them'. The moral tones of the report seem to have had no answer from Australians who have continued to plan their families with care. In recent years Australian women have taken to the Pill far more readily than any other population in the world.

Australia is still sparsely populated by the standards of the world, yet it has some very large cities. There is plenty of scope for future development and its growth rate of 260,000 a year is, in the circumstances, fairly modest. It remains as one of the few havens into which Europeans in search of open space can move.

INDIA—AN UNDERDEVELOPED COUNTRY

India is chosen as a representative of those states in Asia that support the largest populations in the world yet remain predominantly agricultural communities. India, together with Pakistan, China and Indonesia contain over 40 per cent of the world's population and continue to grow at a fast rate. While the population continues to rise at 2 per cent a year or more, there is little chance of these states being able to do more than to keep the extra people alive. As fast as extra food is produced, it is used to support the growing population.

There is little chance of the rapid rate of population growth being halted for at least two generations as the populations of all these countries are particularly young. Even if the size of the average family was to be cut by half over a short period, as happened

Sacred cow. This is a Hindu sacred cow in ceremonial dress. Such cows roam free in Indian towns and villages and make it difficult to breed cattle scientifically. They also trample over the growing crops.

in many European countries, the much larger number of people reaching marriageable age would mean that the number of families would be greatly increased. The population pyramid of India on page 44 shows that in 1961 the 0–4 age group was almost exactly twice the size of the 20–24 age group and is almost bound to produce a very large generation in due time.

It is wrong to think that the food position in these Asian countries has suddenly become worse. It has merely failed to improve. Western Asia and the Indian sub-continent have always supported some of the largest populations in the world at a modest standard of living and this position continues. Population growth has been vigorous for over two centuries, but until recently was subjected to setbacks that are associated with agricultural economies. India suffered from two famines in 1876–8 and 1898–1900 while in 1918 it is estimated that 15 million Indians were killed by the influenza epidemic. These disasters killed off the equivalent of a decade's population growth and kept life expectation in India down to twenty-five years. More recent catastrophes in India have been on a far smaller scale. The Bengal famines of the Second World War, the partition massacres of 1947 and the famines in Bihar in 1966–7 have had no great effect on population growth. The effects of local disasters have been lessened by better medical services and improved famine relief which have given Indians a life expectation of over forty years.

It is the decline in mortality that explains the growth of the Indian population from 248 million in 1921 to just under 500 million in 1966. The Indian population has doubled in forty-five years and it is difficult to see how it can fail to double again before the year 2000, since the next generation is bound to be large and expectation of life will improve further.

It is wrong to think that all India's problems are created by the growth in population. India has a very distinctive way of life which makes change in agricultural method and patterns of work more difficult. Hinduism, the prevailing religion, is a very conservative force with its emphasis on caste. Each Indian is born into a caste which fixes his position in society for life. Some are born to beg, some to labour, some to become shopkeepers and some to be leaders. In these circumstances Indian labour is very immobile. Agriculture is held back by the Hindu veneration of the cow. These creatures are allowed to wander at will, nibbling at the crops, without ever being killed for their meat. The privilege of the cow makes it more difficult for Indian peasants to adopt scientific agricultural methods. There is therefore a certain fatalism in the Indian outlook which makes them slow to adapt to the change which rapid population growth demands.

Indians are unlikely to find an answer to their population problem by the postponement of marriage. Early marriage is a social custom in India, so much so that many children are married before they have reached puberty. There are laws against this custom but they are often ignored. The average marriage age for Indians in 1961 was 15·6 years, which is remarkably young by world standards. Marrying so young has its dangers in the greater difficulty in childbirth, which causes the death of many young Indian mothers. There is also the fact that young widows are strongly discouraged by social custom from marrying again. On balance, therefore, a moderate rise of the marriage age would have little effect on the birth rate. Almost all Indian women enter marriage and a slight delay might actually improve their child-bearing capacity.

The problems presented by the rapid population growth were such that the Indian government decided as early as 1950 that Indian economic development could not be stepped up to the level where it could support the increasing number of people. The Indian government therefore became the first one in the world to adopt a national policy of population limitation by means of family planning. Its efforts started in a small way, but now constitute an important part of the national plan. It has by no means solved the population problem, but it has made significant progress. The fortunes of this and other birth control programmes will be examined in Chapter 7.

Improved Indian farming. This picture illustrates two United Nations agencies co-operating together to solve problems which hamper agricultural improvement in India. The two agencies are the Food and Agricultural Organisation (FAO) and the World Health Organisation (WHO). They are working jointly on the frontier of India and Nepal to bulldoze out the swamps where the malarial mosquito thrives and to prepare the land for rice production.

6 POPULATION AND FOOD SUPPLY

THOMAS MALTHUS

The most famous theory of population was propounded by Thomas Malthus in his *Essay on the Principle of Population* published in 1798. He was writing at a time when the whole pattern of agriculture and industry was beginning to change in England, yet he was more concerned with the growing population. His fear was that population would always tend to press on the available food resources so that the numbers of people at the base of society would always be checked by the vice and misery created by malnutrition. He wrote:

> I believe that it has been very generally remarked by those who have attended to bills of mortality that of the number of children who die annually, much too great a proportion belongs to those who may be supposed unable to give their offspring proper food and attention, exposed as they are occasionally to severe distress and confined, perhaps, to unwholesome habitations and hard labour.

He based his reasoning on two assumptions. First, that food is necessary to the existence of man and secondly, that the passion between the sexes is necessary and will remain nearly in its present state. As far as Malthus could see, if population continued to rise and the desire to reproduce remained constant, population would multiply in a geometrical progression—1, 2, 4, 8, 16, 32 and so on.

Unfortunately it was impossible for the production of food to keep pace with this kind of growth. Food production could only be increased in an arithmetical progression, 1, 2, 3, 4, 5, 6, 7, so that as population increased, the amount of food available to each person would decrease. 'The food which before supported seven millions must now be divided among seven and a half millions or eight millions. The poor consequently must live much worse, and many of them be reduced to severe distress.' Suffering will cause marriages to be delayed, it will cause people to work harder and for lower wages and the consequent cheap labour will encourage farmers to turn up fresh soil and increase output. By these means food production will catch up with population momentarily before the cycle of population growth is again repeated. The cycle of growth, misery and retrenchment was, in Malthus's view, inevitable, unless man could exercise moral restraint, by which he meant

Dr Thomas Malthus (1766–1834). Malthus was a clergyman and a Cambridge don who wrote the famous book on population called *An Essay on the Principle of Population*, first published in 1798.

restraint from sexual intercourse. He at no time advocated birth control by artificial methods, which he would have counted as vice.

As far as England and all other industrialised countries are concerned, Malthus's predictions have proved wrong, for the population in these countries has increased without disastrous famines or epidemics and without hunger among the labouring classes. Production has always kept ahead of population growth and deficiences of food from home production have been made up by imports from abroad. In this way population has increased and the standard of living has improved at the same time in a way that Malthus did not foresee.

Malthus's theory is much more relevant to those countries which have experienced a population rise, yet have retained predominantly agricultural economies, such as India or China. As Malthus demonstrated, agricultural output cannot be suddenly increased in the way that industrial output can. Either new land must be brought under cultivation or more food must be wrung from the soil. Virgin agricultural land no longer exists in the quantities necessary to provide vast new food supplies and the task of making two ears of corn or rice grow where one grew before is both slow and costly. India has been experiencing this predicament, for although it managed to increase annual grain production from 55 to 75 million tons between 1951 and 1966, during the same period the daily food consumption per head dropped from 12·8 oz (362 g) to 12·4 oz (355 g). Even though Indian agriculture was making every effort to produce more food, it was still losing the race to feed the growing population.

WORLD DIET

It is very difficult to measure hunger, which can be a sign of health. It is somewhat easier to assess diet with the modern knowledge of nutrition. It is perfectly possible to be full of food yet badly fed and therefore it is much better to avoid the word hunger in talking of the world food situation. Talk of the 'hungry world' and 'the half of the world that is hungry' is unscientific and emotive. It is only really possible to assess whether a population is badly fed or underfed.

Malnutrition is the condition of being badly fed and is the result of ignorance rather than of food shortage. A balanced diet must contain a number of ingredients. The bulk is provided by carbohydrates, proteins and fats which provide the fuel for the body in the form of heat energy. Carbohydrates are found in the most usual basic foods such as wheat, rice, potatoes and sugar. A diet of carbohydrates alone will satisfy hunger but will not support life. Diet must contain protein, which not only

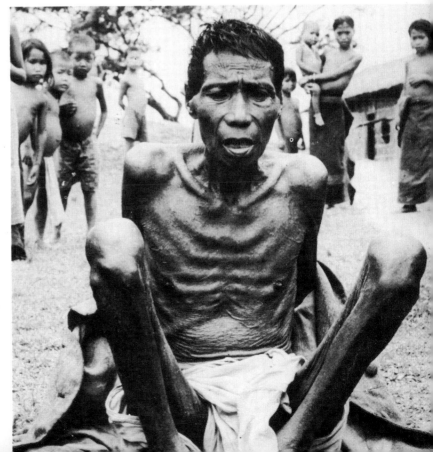

Famine. This old Indian man is suffering from malnutrition and tuberculosis. Disease and hunger tend to go hand in hand.

provides energy but is also necessary for the proper growth and maintenance of the body. Children and pregnant mothers have a special need for it, but all adults need it in small quantities. Fats are not vital to life, but they do provide twice as much energy per pound as protein or carbohydrates and provide a very concentrated form of heat energy. They also help to make food more palatable.

The body needs continual supplies of energy in the form of food to carry out the various functions demanded of it. This energy is measured in calories. The calorific needs of a person vary according to age, weight, environment and activity. People doing hard, physical work in a cold climate need great quantities of food, whilst those who have office jobs in the tropics need very little. The number of calories required by the average person has been assessed at 2,100 calories a day.

Studies of calorie supply in the world made by the Food and Agricultural Organisation (FAO) suggest that in the world as a whole there is an approximate balance between supply and requirements. As would be expected, however, some parts of the world such as Europe and North America have a surplus while the Far East has a deficiency. The Far East supplies all its food, as it cannot afford imports and it can only supply 90 per cent of the requirement suggested by the FAO. This is a very serious deficiency as it occurs in an area which supports a half of the world's population. It has caused some demographers to question the FAO's assessment of basic food requirements, especially for children. If Sri Lankan boys from prosperous homes can live healthily on half of the FAO's requirement and half of what an English boy would require, then it is possible that the problem of undernourishment in the Far East is not as bad as the FAO has suggested. The situation in Africa, Latin America and the Near East is that the food supply almost exactly balances the need.

Most of the countries outside Europe and North America experience the problems created by lack of variety in the diet. The South Eastern Asian diet consists of rice at every meal with flavourings provided mainly by vegetables and sugar. Africans consume large quantities of starchy vegetables like coco yams and cassava. The diet in these areas contains little meat or milk, which are a much richer source of protein than plants or vegetables. Not only is it more difficult to provide the right quantity of protein from a mainly vegetable diet, but there is also a greater danger of failing to provide the vitamins and minerals that are essential to good health. Absence of these will cause deficiency diseases which are still all too common in the world. These ingredients in the diet are only necessary in small quantities and can usually be provided from local sources once the deficiency is understood. Beri-beri was quite common in Asia because the principal food was polished rice. The vitamin B necessary to combat the disease could be supplied once it was understood that the vitamin existed in the husk. Milk and eggs can cure the eye disease called xerophthalmia which occurs in India and is caused by vitamin A deficiency.

(*Opposite*) Intensive farming in China. Members of a Chinese Commune are here seen treating a well-farmed field of wheat with grass ash. It is a typical example of recent Chinese efforts to increase production using the plentiful labour that is available and local raw materials.

There are therefore two parts to the world food problem. The first is malnutrition, which can be solved partly by education and partly by the provision of a greater variety of food. The second is undernutrition which could be solved by better distribution of the available food if that were possible, but could also be solved by improvement of the methods of agricultural production in the countries facing the food shortages.

PRODUCING MORE FOOD

The salvation of the developing countries depends on their ability to feed their growing populations and to free soil for other productive export crops that will raise the general standard of living. In the industrialised countries increased population stimulated agriculture into greater production, which in turn provided more jobs on the land and more food for the towns. The recent population growth in the

developing world has been too rapid to provide surplus food or surplus land. Increased production has tended to be consumed at the local level where the farming methods have barely improved. The extra labour provided by the population growth is not used to any advantage either in the towns or in the countryside. Nothing has happened to galvanise the huge populations into action, except perhaps in China, where there has been a great effort by the Communist government to organise an industrial and an agricultural revolution.

A sign of hope for the countries in this predicament is provided by high-yielding crops. A new variety of wheat was developed by Rockefeller Foundation scientists in Mexico in the late 1950s which helped to triple wheat production in that country by 1967. A similar group of scientists, working through the International Rice Research Institute in the Philippines in the early 1960s, discovered a new 'miracle' rice which could produce twice the yield of other rice strains in Asia. It was called IR-8 and was a cross between a tall rice from Indonesia and a dwarf rice from Taiwan. It grows on a short stalk which enables it to carry the heavy ear. Other hybrid cereals have been developed which are more suitable to other climates and conditions, and these new, high-yield crops are being adopted in much of Asia. By 1969, thirty-four million acres (fourteen million hectares) were planted with these new crops which amounted to one-tenth of the region's total grain area.

The result has been a sudden improvement in the production of certain cereals, which provides a chance for the developing nations to provide for their own food needs and leave some to spare. Pakistan increased its wheat harvest by just under 60 per cent between 1967 and 1969 and Indian wheat production increased by 50 per cent between 1965 and 1969. The kind of effect that this 'yield take off' has at local level can be illustrated from the Northern Punjab, where the wage rate for farm labourers went up by 40 per cent between 1965 and 1968. There was a shortage of labour because the new cereals demand much higher provision of water and fertilisers. New farming methods also encourage the idea of growing two crops in one year, a process which is called double-cropping. In fact, Indian farmers are now able to produce three crops every fourteen months using intensive irrigation systems and ample fertilisers.

The success of the 'yield take off' in Asia has taken the marketing system by surprise. It is no easy task to find outlets for surplus food on the world market as the Philippines have found to their cost. Surplus food is useless unless it can be turned into real income for other purposes. Mexico provides a success story in this respect as the Mexicans have managed to sell part of their increased wheat production with benefit to the whole economy. It is also essential that the farmers receive a good price for their products. Some countries, like India, have been following cheap food

(*Left*) High-yield rice. This experimental farm in the Philippine Islands is one where ways to improve rice production are sought. High-yield rice strains need plenty of fertiliser and this experiment is to discover how this expensive commodity can be used most efficiently.

(*Right*) Old and new rice compared. Hybrid varieties of rice have been developed in a number of Far Eastern countries. They bear heavier yields and are suitable for double cropping. This picture compares the rice CO23, traditionally grown in Southern India, with the high-yield hybrid rice, IR5. The new types of rice have greatly boosted rice production.

policies to enable poor people to afford it. It is done by beating down the price that the farmers receive for their product and the effect is to discourage them from investing in greater food production. The new high-yield crops mean that much more money has to be spent, long before any profit can be made. This money is used to provide the special seed, the fertilisers, the irrigation system and the extra labour. Farmers will only take the risk involved if the financial reward is attractive.

The increase in food production will not solve any problems by itself. It can change things if it has a stimulating effect on other productive activities. The increased production of grain demands the construction of new granaries and storage facilities so that the loss to birds, rodents and insects will be minimised. The demand for fertilisers and water provides other work opportunities. The need for extra labour in the fields holds out the chance of better-paid jobs. Sale of surplus food abroad will help to buy foreign goods. All this should provide many people with a more dignified way of life and once people have dignity they begin to think more carefully about the quality of their children's upbringing. This is what happened in the West and the effect was to encourage smaller families.

Another possibility is that the increased availability of food will merely encourage further population growth at the same level of destitution. If this happens, a golden opportunity will have been missed and it will be even more difficult to solve the world population problem should yet another breakthrough in food production occur in the future.

(*Below left*) An Israeli kibbutz has been built in the wilderness to wrest crops from the desert. A kibbutz is a collective farm, where the whole community plans the campaign together and carries it through in an orderly way. In this way land which was once arid is beginning to produce ample food.

(*Below*) The main meal of the day in Britain (on the right) and Brazil (on the left). The British meal of boiled ham explains itself. The Brazil Indians feed off a cake made of baked vegetables which will be spread with a fish paste.

LAND USE

Concentration has been centred so far on Asia because the problem of overpopulation, which Asian countries have faced for the last twenty or thirty years, consumes public interest. There is so little good agricultural land left for exploitation in Eastern Asia that man really seems to be reaching his maximum numbers, in that area at least. The problem of underpopulation in Africa and South America receives far less publicity. The standard of living of the African or South American Indian is just as low as his Asian equivalent and the rate of population growth is as fast or rather faster. For instance, there is no country in Central America which has a current growth rate below 3 per cent per year, and the population is extremely young, with between 42 and 51 per cent of the population in the 0–14 age group. In these circumstances it is forecast that the present population of Latin America, which stands at 263 million people may treble before the end of the century. This is the area of fastest population growth in the world.

There is clearly room for the opening up of empty areas in both Latin America and Africa. Population density in Latin America as a whole is relatively low at 20·4 people to the square mile (7·8 people per square kilometre) as compared with 50·5 in the USA and 560 in the United Kingdom. At the moment the cost of preparing new land for agriculture exceeds the profit which can be harvested from it, but this need not always be so. There are also the difficulties and dangers of bringing tropical jungle into cultivation to be considered. The traditional method of cutting down the forest and burning the wood to provide an ash soil is primitive, inefficient and potentially damaging. The soil quickly turns to dust when exposed to the sun and is easily washed away into the rivers. Tropical agriculture will need to be developed with great care or cool forests will be turned into torrid deserts. The first improvement in Latin America will be made on the existing farmland which is inefficiently used in many cases. The large estates of the grandees will need to be opened up to more extensive exploitation and the peasants will have to be persuaded to consolidate their tiny farms into larger profitable holdings.

Africa is in a similar position to Latin America as far as population development is concerned. The population of tropical and north Africa is growing at about 3 per cent each year which is as fast as anywhere in the world. The continent can support a much larger population, but so much of the area is jungle or desert that it can only be successfully exploited by the application of science and capital. The irony is that the chance of educating the African children becomes worse the more there are of them. Nevertheless there is a good deal of optimism in a country like Tanzania, a country of more than ten million people, who live at a density of 30 to the square mile (11·5 per square kilometre). President Nyerere declared in 1967 in a famous speech outlining his plans for Tanzania,

A great part of Tanzania's land is fertile and gets sufficient rains. Our country can produce various crops for home consumption and for export. We can produce food crops such as maize, rice, wheat, beans and groundnuts, which can be exported if produced in large quantities. And we can produce such cash crops as sisal, cotton, coffee, tobacco, pyrethrum and tea.

There is enough slack both in the underexploitation of existing land and in the reservoir of virgin land for a larger population to be provided with sufficient food, but at the present rates of growth, the empty spaces of Africa and Latin America will soon be filled.

(*Opposite*) Deficiency disease. This little boy from Guatemala is a victim of kwashiorkor, which is caused by a deficiency of vitamins. The spots on the face are typical of the disease which is widespread in the tropics and sub-tropics among children. It disappears if there is enough milk, meat and eggs in the child's diet.

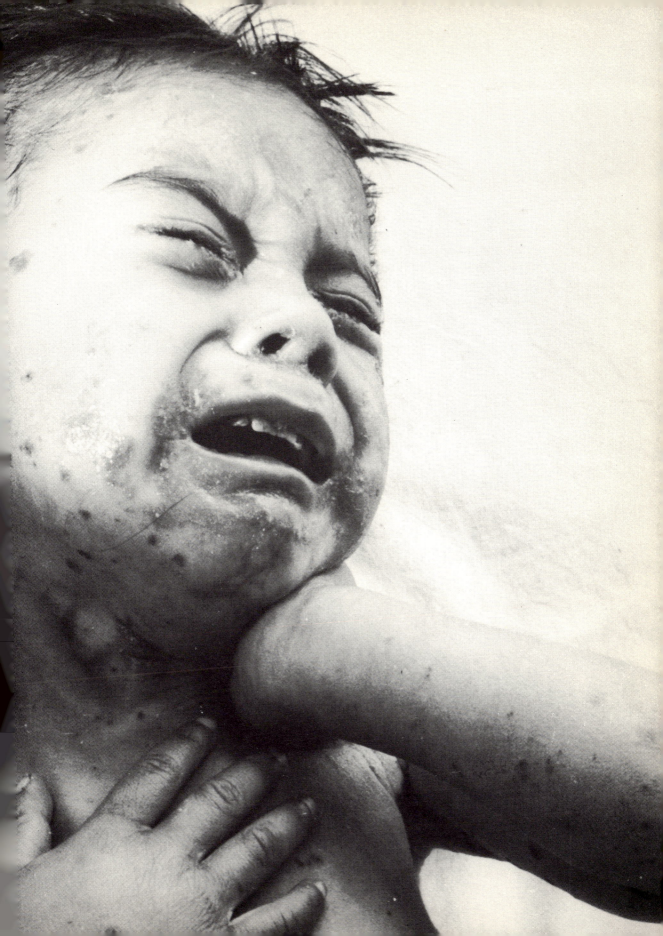

7 POPULATION POLICIES

Population control is not a new concept. The killing of infants, which is called infanticide, is a crude but effective method of keeping population under control. This was practised not only in primitive societies but also by the Greeks and Romans and more recently by the Japanese. The killing of infants is no longer legal but the killing of the unborn child, which is called abortion, is becoming much more acceptable throughout the world.

The encouragement of population growth also has a long history. Boy children have almost always been valued as potential soldiers and have tended to be more valued than girls, but the need for them has led societies to encourage large families. States began to encourage large families when kings built up strong states in Europe in the late seventeenth and early eighteenth centuries. Louis xiv of France, through his controller general of finance, Colbert, encouraged certain of his subjects to have large families; the nobles as the potential warrior class, and the craftsmen as the basis of industrial growth. Tax exemption was offered to taxpayers with more than ten children and pensions to nobles with families of similar size. The kings of Prussia (previously the electors of Brandenburg) attempted to solve their need for soldiers and craftsmen more quickly by encouraging immigration. More recently, policies encouraging faster population growth have been less usual, but were favoured by dictators like Hitler who believed wholeheartedly in the superiority of the German race. They have also been pursued by France which had such a low birth rate in comparison to its neighbours in the nineteenth century.

Most developed states have no desire either to encourage or to discourage births. Especially in the free world, decisions on family size are seen to be part of the freedom of man and the job of governments is merely to ensure that all children born have an equal chance in life. Systems of state welfare clearly have a bearing on population patterns, but so far their aim has not been to influence family size in any drastic way. It is in the underdeveloped world that population control is being adopted as a vital part of state planning for the future. Population growth has been so rapid in Asia, Africa and South America that it has become a danger to the successful development of the industrial and agricultural potential of those countries. Not all countries have adopted birth control programmes. Some recognise that rapid population growth

Free milk. Milk provides children with a balanced food which will save them from many deficiency diseases. A Milk in Schools Scheme was launched by the Milk Marketing Board in Britain in 1934. Under this scheme milk was made available to children at school at a reduced price, allowing one-third of a pint per child. After 1946 the milk was provided free by the government, but this concession has now been withdrawn for all children over infant school age. A similar scheme was launched in part of India under the Anand Co-operative Milk Scheme in 1958.

Social welfare. Lloyd George, a member of Asquith's Liberal Government, was largely instrumental in introducing the British system of social welfare before the First World War. National Insurance, pensions and labour exchanges all date from this time. Modern schemes for social insurance against accident, sickness and old age had been introduced even earlier by Bismarck in Germany between 1883 and 1889. The system of national insurance has subsequently been extended in both countries to cover all citizens from the cradle to the grave. It has been copied by many advanced countries, but not by all. The United States of America still upholds that it is an invasion of man's liberty to force him to join a state insurance scheme – a view which would evidently have been shared by this cartoonist.

"OLIVER ASKS FOR" LESS.

JOHN BULL (*fed up*). "PLEASE, SIR, NEED I HAVE QUITE SO MANY GOOD THINGS?"
MR. LLOYD GEORGE. "YES, YOU MUST; AND THERE'S MORE TO COME."

has its advantages where labour is short and land is unoccupied. Others are held back by the religious or moral convictions of some churches.

Population control therefore raises a number of considerations which need to be explored.

THE WELFARE STATE

A welfare state is one that looks after its citizens from the cradle to the grave. The aim is to ensure that everyone enjoys a minimum standard of wealth, housing, education and social security. The state supports the birth of children through maternity allowances and subsidised medical and hospital care. In the nurture of the young the state offers support to the mother in the form of either a weekly monetary grant called the family allowance or a lump sum endowment grant. The father is given tax concessions as compensation for the cost of bringing up children. Systems of family support like this are in operation in almost every developed nation except for the United States where it is presumed that all citizens will provide for their own social security.

Family allowances are a recognition that the bearing of children is not only a response to a basic urge to become a parent, but also a service to the community. Such allowances are rarely paid for the first child, who is the fulfilment of parental ambitions. The second and subsequent children, however, are counted as an extra burden undertaken by the parents, which will help to sustain the national population. Once women are educated to the same standard as men and are free to work on an equal basis with men, as is becoming the case in some Western and Communist countries, it is only right that those mothers who bear more children and tie themselves to the home should be given financial support.

The institution of family allowances on a wide scale occurred after the Second World War at a time when there was a revival of the birth rate in the developed countries. It would, however, be hasty to argue that the allowances caused an increase in births. Extra wages were paid to French workers with families after the First World War without any discernible effect on family size and the New Zealand birth rate did not begin to rise until after the Second World War, even though a system of family allowances was introduced in 1926. Sweden, which has had one of the most advanced family support systems since 1937 has had an annual birth rate which has never risen above twenty per 1,000 since 1922.

The system of welfare support may in fact have an opposite effect. By contributing to the security and dignity of families, it helps to increase their expectations, which in turn suppresses their desire for more children. Those who think that families of more than three children should be penalised by the withdrawal of the family allowance for the fourth and subsequent children or by tax penalties, may well be suggesting a false remedy. If you plunge families into poverty and despair, they may lose the incentive to prevent the birth of further children.

The increase of the proportion of old age pensioners in the population, which is happening in a number of European countries, also creates problems. If old age pensions are financed by a levy through taxation on the working age groups, then the burden of the old will increase as their proportion increases. Trade unions are unwilling to accept increased taxation without increased wages. The grant of increased wages has an inflationary effect, which hits the old age pensioner whose

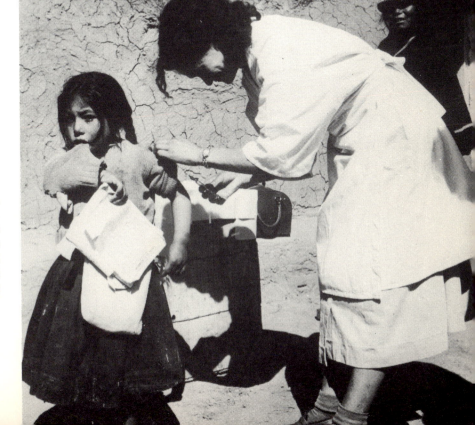

World Health Organisation (WHO) in South America. This is a health centre by the side of Lake Titicaca on the frontier between Peru and Bolivia. The doctors and nurses in the centre were sent out by WHO.

pension loses value. It therefore becomes very difficult to support old age pensioners at an acceptable standard of living.

Another solution to the problem of the old is to raise the age of retirement. Some people who are forced to retire at the age of sixty-five in England would be only too willing to continue work. Work makes them feel wanted and useful. Others see rest from daily work as a privilege which they earn and should be given as early as possible. Early retirement is also supported by the unions, who see an extension of the working life as equivalent to an increase in the working population, which will have the effect of keeping down wages. The real issue, which will become more and more obvious as the proportion of old people increases, is that the longer people continue working, the larger the pension that the state will be able to offer them. Sweden has already taken action in this respect by making sixty-seven the lowest pensionable age. Care will have to be taken that the promotion of younger people is not blocked, but otherwise a longer working life would seem to be one answer to an ageing community.

POLICIES ENCOURAGING BIRTHS

It was in France that welfare policies always had a motive of increasing population. Before the First World War little was done by the French state but private industrialists vied with each other to pay family allowances with wages. A society was also founded by Dr J. Berthillon called the National Alliance for the Increase of the French Population which helped to establish a commission in 1902 on population decline in France. Berthillon had some very striking ideas for encouraging large families such as reserving the highest government posts for members of families of three or more children as well as the more obvious ones.

After 1918 it was again some private employers who fostered the idea of larger cash payments to workers with young families, but in 1932 this was adopted by the government and extended to all industries and occupations. This financial incentive had little effect on French population which was the same size in 1939 as it had been in 1918 and this position of equilibrium was only achieved with the aid of massive immigration. The revival of the French birth rate then occurred in the wake of the *Code de la Famille* of 1939 and the fall of France in 1940. The basis of the system enshrined in the *Code* remained the family allowance financed by levies on industry, but in addition, cash grants were offered to mothers at home caring for children and the cash allowances for fourth and subsequent children were increased. A French worker with a family of four could more than double his income.

The French birth rate has increased since the war but it would be wrong to attribute this to state policy. Many European governments experienced similar rises in the 1940s as part of the general recovery from the depression of the inter-war years. The French rise was more impressive merely because it had been awaited for so much longer.

The USSR has been interested in maintaining a healthy birth rate since the Bolshevik Revolution. It was the cities that began to experience a fall in the birthrate in the

(*Opposite*) Shanty town in South America. These shanty huts built of matted palm have no sanitation, no lighting and no water supply. The squalid surroundings provide fine breeding places for disease. This picture is taken in the suburbs of Lima, the capital of Peru. Similar scenes could be found in the suburbs of Indian cities.

inter-war years and this was worrying to a state which was so sparsely populated by European standards. The Communist government in Russia had encouraged women to work on equal terms with men and therefore the Russian mothers needed help with looking after their children if they were to contemplate larger families. The Russian government allocated money to working mothers for the care of their children as part of a far-reaching population growth policy started in 1936. Kindergartens and child-care centres were started near the factories, generous maternity leave was granted to working mothers and big annual allowances were given to mothers of six or more children. This growth policy was given a new impetus by the Supreme Soviet in 1944, to compensate for the enormous losses that the Russian

population had sustained during the war against Hitler which started for Russia in 1941. The main new ingredient of the 1944 edict was that mothers of large families were to be given medals and honours. For a family of ten children, the mother was to be made a member of the Order of Mother Heroine with a gold medal and a scroll. The policy had no great effect as the Russian birth rate dropped from 40 births per 1,000 people in 1939 to 17·5 per 1,000 in 1967.

The Nazi Party followed more sinister population growth policies during Hitler's regime. It was an increase of the pure German race called the Aryans that he wanted to encourage and rewards were offered according to the purity of the parents' blood. Marriage loans of 1,000 marks were given to sound Aryans and this would never have to be repaid if four children were produced within eight years. These loans were granted in addition to family allowances which were started in 1920 during the Weimar Republic, which preceded Hitler's regime. By 1939, they were also awarding medals to mothers of more than four children. These measures seemed to have their effect as the German birth rate increased from 14·7 births per 1,000 people per year in 1933 to 20·3 in 1939.

It is always considered that the policy of the Roman Catholic Church is to encourage births. It is the only large branch of the Christian Church to oppose the use of contraceptives now and it is one of the few religious groups anywhere to oppose contraceptives on moral grounds. The Catholic Church is not, however, against family limitation or birth control as long as it is achieved by natural means. The most recent definitive statement on the Catholic Church's attitude was published by Pope Paul VI in the papal encyclical, *Humanae Vitae*, published in 1968. This stated:

> If therefore, there are reasonable grounds for spacing births, arising from the physical or psychological condition of husband or wife . . . the Church teaches then that married people may take advantage of the natural cycles immanent in the reproductive system and use their marriage at precisely those times that are infertile and in this way control birth.

Family planning by moral restraint and by use of the 'safe' period is therefore recognised by the Church.

It is clear that many Catholics find the restraints imposed by the Church too demanding and use other contraceptive methods. Dependence on the rhythm of the body is also notoriously risky and is inclined to lead to unwanted pregnancies. An American study has estimated that the rhythm method is half as effective as the widely used condoms and diaphragms. It is this rather than any desire for population growth that accounts for the larger average size of Catholic families compared to Protestant ones.

BIRTH CONTROL POLICIES

A number of governments in underdeveloped countries have formulated national family planning programmes to try to lessen the rate of population growth. Policies of this kind are administered in India, Pakistan, Sri Lanka, Hong Kong, Malaysia, Nepal, Singapore, Thailand and Turkey. Most of the countries which have adopted

Demonstrating for Women's Lib in France. Women have begun to demand greater equality in the working world and this involves the relinquishment of part of their traditional role in the home. Few women are prepared to rear very large families and therefore require medical help to control birth. Demonstrations in Italy in 1971 specifically demanded the legalisation of birth control. It was only in that year that Italian laws forbidding the spread of information on birth control and the sale of contraceptives were repealed. It is still forbidden under Roman Catholic Church Law.

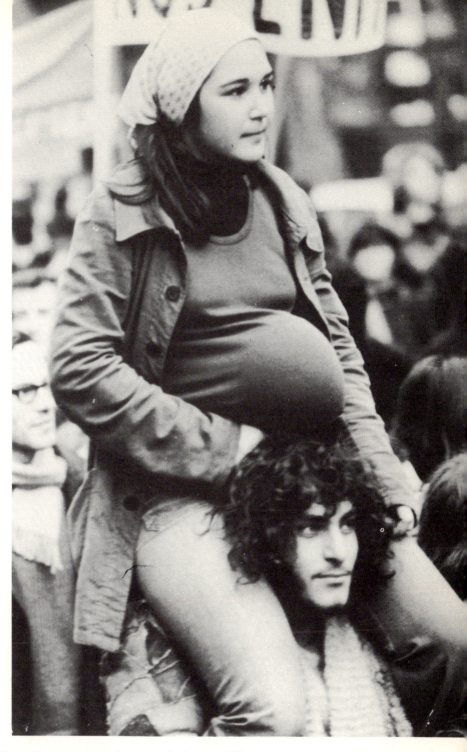

such policies are in Asia where the most pressing population problem exists. All the most highly populated countries have birth control policies although little is known about the Chinese programme. The movement towards birth control has spread so widely that 80 per cent of the people in Asia live under governments that have accepted a responsibility for limiting births.

The first country to start a birth control policy was India in 1950. At first little money was invested in the policy, though the money was wisely spent on research, experiment and tests to assess attitudes. Subsequently the amount of money given to the programme was increased from the original allocation of 330 thousand dollars for the first five-year plan in 1951, to 306 million dollars for the fourth five-year plan in 1966.

The dramatic increase in Indian determination to tackle the problem can be attributed to the United Nations Technical Assistance Mission which was invited to suggest ways of improving the efficiency and effectiveness of the Indian birth control plans of 1963. The Mission reported that the spirit of the plans was admirable, but that it would be impossible to implement without a great increase in the number of doctors, nurses and teachers. Indians would have to be taught carefully in the use of contraceptives and it was this work that would require a large labour force of qualified people. It was felt that the loop would be an acceptable device to Indian women, seeing how readily it had been accepted in Taiwan and South Korea. Condoms should be made more readily available and India should persist with the sterilisation programme.

Chinese communes. The picture shows a band of children from a new commune in Kwantung province. It was built in a desolate area that began to bear crops.

Indian males had proved much more ready to take advantage of free sterilisation than in other countries. The Indian government had already carried out a substantial number during the second five-year plan. They had overcome reluctance through special camps, where fears were soothed away, and by offering a prize of ten rupees (50p) or a transistor radio. Over half the patients already had families of four or more children so the effect of this part of the programme was merely to stop the extension of already large families. The operation, which is called vasectomy, can be carried out in the birth control clinics under a local anaesthetic and does not involve any hospital admission. It was therefore planned that the sterilisation campaign should be greatly extended.

The Mission assessed that an energetic programme could reduce the Indian birth rate in ten years and in 1966 the Indian government began to work towards this target. A Cabinet Committee on Family Planning had already been appointed and its powers extended to all the states in India. The annual targets for loop insertions and vasectomies have proved a little too ambitious, but not badly so. It is estimated that about a million births were prevented in 1967, which is a significant achievement, but the hope is that 85 million births will have been prevented by the end of the ten years, which implies that the effort will have to be greatly increased. The most urgent need is still for trained personnel.

There are aid organisations that offer help in this direction. The United Nations is very keen to assist through its Specialised Agencies and in 1966 the General Assembly of the United Nations unanimously supported an extension of the work of the Economic and Social Council in the field of population control. Private organisations in America, such as the Ford Foundation and the Population Council, which was founded by John Rockefeller, support research on birth control procedures. The Population Council developed the modern form of the intra-uterine device, the IUD, and it allows governments of underdeveloped countries to manufacture it.

By far the largest contribution by outside agencies is made by the United States Agency for International Development (AID), which was founded on the recommendation of the Draper Commission of 1959. Its activities were quickened after it had been placed under the office of the War on Hunger by President Johnson in 1967. The aim of AID is not to persuade foreign governments to initiate birth control policies but to offer help in money, advice and equipment to those countries that have such policies already.

The effort to control the growth of population by a mammoth programme of social engineering has only been mounted with any determination since 1966 and it is therefore too early to assess how valuable it has been. The little information that is available gives strong hints of success. There does not seem to be any great opposition from the public to the programmes. The only major religious groups to oppose birth control are the Roman Catholics and the Buddhists. Lack of general education and basic hygiene do not seem insuperable obstacles to the acceptance of the birth control equipment. The problem is therefore really one of planning, finance and education. If a high enough priority is given to population control in national planning, there seems no reason why dramatic falls in the birth rate cannot be achieved through government action. Significant falls have already been achieved in Taiwan, Singapore and Hong Kong and it is to be hoped that similar falls can be achieved in larger countries such as India and Pakistan.

The picture shows a more traditional Chinese scene in another commune on the Chiangan Plain in Central China. It is in the middle of an important rice-growing area and this is the threshing season.

8 POPULATION AND THE FUTURE

Demographers have very opposed ideas about the future of world population. The more pessimistic feel that the world is already on the verge of a catastrophe, due to growing overcrowding, pressure on resources and the unbalancing of the delicate equilibrium that enables life to survive on earth. At the other extreme there are optimists who feel that the world is nowhere near the optimum population and that the present rapid increase is just a passing phase.

There are reasons to suppose that the recent upsurge in population is a unique event caused by the medical advances of the last two hundred years. These benefits have only been available on a world-wide scale for the last thirty years or so and the effect has been to increase life expectancy enormously. Babies have a good chance of survival all over the world and once they survive infancy, they can expect to live to

Torrey Canyon Disaster. A giant oil tanker, the *Torrey Canyon*, was shipwrecked on the Seven Stones Reef off Cornwall, England in March 1967. Crude oil was deposited in large quantities on the Cornish beaches and it had to be sprayed painstakingly with detergent.

forty at least. Death no longer controls numbers to any degree and it is some time before alternative methods of control are adopted by society. Experience shows that an improved standard of living or a higher level of education does gradually affect family size, but it would be wrong to expect it to happen without human effort.

The present experience of many Asian countries is that population is rising so fast that society has not had time to adapt its customs to the new situation by natural means. Science has unbalanced population by saving life and it seems logical that science should find ways of restoring the balance. Some demographers think that science applied by governments cannot change breeding habits or family size by birth control policies. They can only do it by changing the social climate through education and economic advance.

This is to argue from the experience of history, for all successful limitations of family size seem to have been in response to social and economic pressures. There is also a close link between family size and the length of education that the parents have experienced. Yet the general acceptance and use of contraceptive devices is such a recent phenomenon that it is difficult to provide any useful information about the effect of their general use on population. It is also impossible to estimate the effect of government propaganda on family patterns, as the modern instruments of mass communication are so much more powerful and effective than anything known in the past. Films, television and radio may well overcome the difficulties of trying to spread new ideas among illiterate people. There are also very few religious or moral organisations which condemn birth control practices. The way seems clear for successful birth control campaigns.

If the birth rate can be moderated at a time when food production is increasing rapidly, then an improvement in the standard of life and of education will become possible. This in turn may persuade people to limit family size as it did in the West. The opportunity provided by dramatically increased food production must be seized at once. If it merely serves to support a continually expanding population, then nature will provide its own checks of famine and plague as Malthus predicted. Population cannot go on increasing indefinitely without the intervention of such drastic checks. The desirable effect of a reduction in births is that it frees money that might have been invested in houses and schools for investment in machinery and greater production.

THE WORLD POPULATION PROBLEM

The most pessimistic views about the future of world population come from America, which is both very rich and also lightly populated by world standards. The United States has no population policy in the Asian sense. It now has a population of just over 200 million people in a country with an area of just under 3 million square miles (4·8 million square kilometres). This constitutes a density which is only about one-tenth that of Great Britain. There are massive surpluses of food and a great wealth of raw materials within the frontiers. Yet some American demographers and sociologists advocate not just a moderation of the birth rate, but an actual stop in

National Park, Utah. Pressure on living space is such that wilderness has to be set aside for man's enjoyment. This is part of the Bryce Canyon National Park in Utah, USA.

population growth. They want to reach a position of zero growth very quickly because they see further population increase as a hazard to the environment on the earth.

The difficulty from the American point of view, and from the European point of view to a lesser extent, is the expectation of every baby born. Americans enjoy such a high standard of living that they consume much more per head of the population than anywhere else in the world. Every American born will probably have as his goal the possession of cars, a boat, electronic equipment, a fine house, a swimming pool, all of which eat up the irreplacable resources of the world. The world can only support a limited number of people at this kind of standard because there are limits to what the earth can produce. It may be possible to support the present world population of 3,000 million people at the American standard of living, but it would not be possible to support double that number, which seems to be an inevitable prospect.

It takes very little to support an Indian child. He can expect very few belongings during his life and can look forward to a very scant diet. The Indian way of life is basically simple and even if the wealth of the average Indian is increased it is unlikely that he will demand the extra cars, the cameras, the boats and push-button appliances that make up the sophisticated civilisation of the West. It is to be hoped that other areas of the world like Africa and Latin America will avoid the worst excesses of the Western emphasis on consumption and on mass production that has been the ingredient of Western civilisation in the last one hundred years. Only if the various parts of the world retain their own unique characteristics will it remain an interesting place. By preserving the simplicity of life in the greater part of the world, the burden of population on resources will be avoided and there will be room for many more people.

The population problem is different in the various parts of the world. The American problem is how to accommodate a modest population at a very high standard of living in a political system which does not allow the central government to plan the use of resources of oil, water and land to any great extent. The Western European problem is how to accommodate a large population in a limited area without losing the basic amenities of a pleasant life, such as open countryside, wildlife and clean surroundings. The problem in the Third World, as the developing countries are called, is how to raise the growing population from a life of wretchedness to one of dignity.

It is misleading, therefore, to talk of the world population problem as if it were a single problem. It is also misleading to associate other problems with population as if population growth was the root of all evil. Dangers to the soil from pesticides or from soil erosion, dangers to the air, the rivers and the seas from pollution or threats to life on earth caused by the sources of power which drive our machines and so heat the atmosphere, are caused by the carelessness of man's exploitation of his environment. Since the Industrial Revolution first began, man has been exploiting the earth without regard to future consequences. His ability to do this has been an indication of underpopulation and plenty. The position has now been reached where there is very little land or sea that can be exploited without harming the interests of other people and the hope is that it will lead to a more orderly development of the raw materials of the land and sea. Some people are trying to restore the balance of nature by returning to the countryside and cottage crafts, but this is perhaps too romantic. A more realistic use of modern technology and science is to aim for improvements which turn desert into fertile land, as has happened in Israel, or sea into land, as has happened in Holland. These improvements tend to be made where population is plentiful rather than where it is sparse. Moderate population growth is not a threat to man's future: it is a spur to his ingenuity.

(*Opposite*) Polluted river. A little poison in a river can kill off the whole local fish population in a very short time with ugly results. Dirty rivers soon lose certain species of fish and will eventually die completely.

PROJECTIONS OF WORLD POPULATION

The Population Branch of the Department of Economic and Social Affairs of the UN makes periodic forecasts of population. It does not make any firm predictions, but suggests a number of possible world population sizes depending on the success of schemes to bring population under control. If birth rates remain as they are at present and if life expectation continues to increase by six months each year, then the population of the world will increase from 2,998 million people in 1960 to 7,522 million in 2000. This figure is very unlikely to be reached by 2000 as there has been such a marked move towards population control in the late 1960s in underdeveloped countries. President Nixon was reflecting a similar mood of concern in America

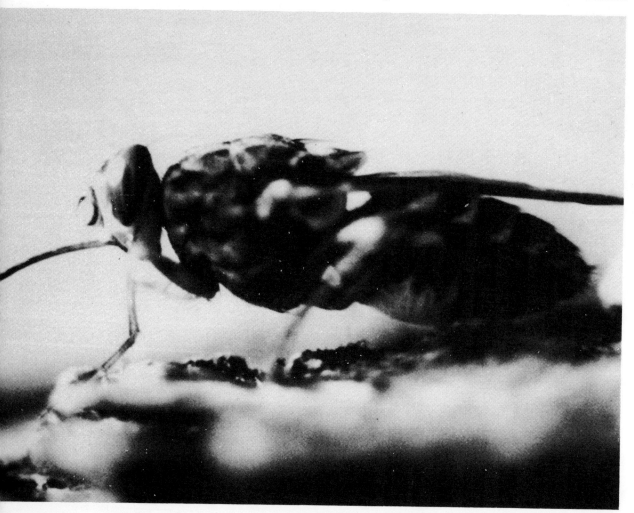

The tsetse fly. A female tsetse fly, gorged with blood, rests upon the branch of a mopani tree in East Africa. Tsetses do not lay eggs, but deposit their full-grown larvae alive in the skin of animals – one every eleven days. The tough proboscis, which is hollow like a straw, can penetrate the hide of an elephant. The affected animal develops sleeping sickness, which causes yearly losses in African livestock amounting to millions of pounds.

when he spoke to Congress in 1969 of the difficulties of coping with such a rapid increase, which would take the United States from 200 million to 300 million by the turn of the century. He said 'this growth will produce serious challenges for our society. Many of our present social problems may be related to the fact that we have had only fifty years to accommodate the second hundred million Americans'. The assumption in America is that the central government will have to influence opinion in the direction of birth control.

The United Nations' Report thought that the most likely world population in 2000 would be 6,130 millions. This figure assumes that birth control policies will be successful enough to prevent over one thousand million births. It still constitutes a growth rate of 2 per cent per year which is a little higher than it is at present. The reason why growth will be so fast is that world population at the moment has a very low average age and vast numbers will be reaching marriageable age in the next forty years. The chances are that the average age of the world population will have increased by AD 2000 and therefore the birth rate will decline.

The population projection for the various parts of the world will be as follows:

Estimate of world population in millions

	1960 (actual)	1980	2000
North America	199	262	354
Europe	425	479	527
Russia	214	278	353
Australia	16	23	32
Asia	1659	2461	3458
Africa	273	449	768
Latin America	212	378	638
Total	2998	4330	6130

It can be seen from these figures that Europe is growing at by far the slowest rate, followed by America and Russia. All the other areas more than double their totals. Changes in the balance of numbers of the world on this scale is bound to lead to shifts in the centres of power and influence, especially if the huge populations can be mobilised into productive economic activity.

It is also a sobering thought that it will take modern man a mere forty years to double the number of people living on the earth, when it took all of man's existence on earth, perhaps a million years, to reach the present number. This feat is a triumph for human knowledge and a victory of man over his environment, but it is a success which raises thought about the total capacity of the earth to support life, for this would be the ultimate limiting factor in population growth.

THE OPTIMUM POPULATION

The word 'optimum' means the most favourable, or best, and involves value judgements about man's role on the earth. Many would consider that the most favourable population size has already been passed in many countries. Others would consider that the industrial society based on huge cities is too high a price to pay for population growth. What is really involved in considering the limits of population growth is the maximum population and in this consideration the main limiting factors are food, water and air. Water and oxygen are in plentiful supply, but could be dissipated by certain industrial and agricultural practices. Only about 5 per cent of the water used is consumed by humans. The rest is utilised in industrial processes for cooling or in agriculture for irrigation. There should never be a lack of water for drinking. The burning of fossil fuels such as coal and oil has raised the carbon dioxide content of the atmosphere by 12 per cent in the last 150 years. It may become necessary to conserve the oxygen in the atmosphere which we breathe by switching over to nuclear and solar energy.

It is now generally accepted that the capacity of the earth to produce food has been underestimated. Shortage of food is unlikely to be a constraint on population during the present phase of population growth. It has been estimated that for an American-type diet, given the most efficient systems of farming, the land requirement would be 2,000 square metres (half an acre) for every person, with an extra 250

Spun protein chunks. This kind of food protein can be manufactured from basic raw materials by industrial processes. Unappetising protein sources such as soya beans can be reconstituted to look like meat. These have a very high food value and are already marketed.

square metres to supply American needs in timber. If this is set against the agricultural potential of the world, with double-cropping where the land is suitable, the world could support a population of 47,000 million people, compared to the present population of 3,000 million. If, on the other hand, the world population was to subsist on the basic diet mainly of cereals common in Asia today, the maximum figure would be closer to 470,000 million.

These calculations suggest that other limitations on population size will intervene before such figures are reached. Animal populations in the state of nature experience rapid growth from time to time and their progress is ultimately checked by shortage of space, accumulation of waste products and shortage of food. Man is obviously capable of foreseeing the problems of space and waste and of solving them. It is possible, however, that city life will in the end sap man's morale, for he is becoming increasingly a city dweller. Cities tend to grow so fast that planners are always solving the last problem while the next is threatening the city's future. Social problems like poverty and deprivation tend to fester in the centre of cities where they could be organised into a potent political force. The servicing of a city with power, food and transport is so complex that mechanical or human failures can threaten the comfort of many. It is the ever-growing complexity of the industrial communities, some of which could not feed themselves without trade, that makes them vulnerable. Economics which are based more firmly on agriculture and rural crafts may finally prove longer lasting.

Hong Kong. The 1959 population was 2,806,000 in an area of 391 square miles (1013 square kilometres). The density is therefore 7,200 people to the square mile (about 2,770 to the square kilometre) and it continues to grow with migration from mainland China.

BOOK LIST

The study of population can start at a local level by consulting the census returns in the local library. In the United Kingdom, the results of each census are published in several volumes. The results of the 1961 census have all been published as have the results of the sample census of 1966. The results of the 1971 census are beginning to appear. Local libraries should have all volumes covering the United Kingdom. They should also have the area reports covering the library's locality and neighbouring counties. The Registrar General publishes annually a statistical review and annual estimates of the population of England and Wales (HMSO).

On a world scale the best reference source is the United Nations Demographic Yearbook published by the UN Department of Economic and Social Affairs.

There are some important books that should be mentioned on the theory of population. These are rather technical for beginners.

Demography
Demography, P. R. Cox (Cambridge University Press).
Population Facts and Methods of Demography, N. Keyfitz and W. Flieger (W. H. Freeman).

Population Theory
An Essay on the Principle of Population, T. R. Malthus (Pelican).
General Theory of Population, Alfred Sauvy (Weidenfeld and Nicolson).

The following books are recommended for class use:
History of Population
The Economic History of World Population, Carlo Cipolla (Pelican).
Poverty, Graeme Kent, Past-into-Present Series (Batsford).
Population and History, E. A. Wrigley (Weidenfeld and Nicolson).
Children, David Kennedy Past-into-Present Series (Batsford).

Population Control
Population Control, edited by A. Allison (Pelican).
The Growth and Control of Population, W. D. Borrie (Weidenfeld and Nicolson).
Conservation and Pollution, Olive Jackson, World Wide Series (Batsford).

Population and Food Supply
Seeds of Change – the green revolution in the 1970s, L. R. Brown (Pall Mall Press).
Population Growth and Land Use, C. G. Clark (Macmillan).
Population Bomb, P. Ehrlich (Ballantine).
World Food, Nance Lui Fyson, World Wide Series (Batsford).
World Poverty, Paul Henderson, World Wide Series (Batsford).
Born to Hunger, A. Hopcraft (Heinemann).
World Population and Food Supply, J. H. Lowry (Edward Arnold).

General
Population, R. K. Kelsall (Longman).
The Population of Britain, T. K. Robinson (Longman).

INDEX

The numbers **in bold type** refer to the pages on which illustrations appear